To Barry,
Happy Christmas

GW00384852

Pacific Avengers

by Mike Roussel

The story of a Fleet Air Arm pilot's training and service with 857 Squadron in the British Pacific Fleet.

Best Regards,
Mike Roussel

Published by
Little Knoll Press
First published – September 2015

ISBN No. 978-0-9927220-7-4

Copies of this book can be obtained
by emailing Jenny@LittleKnollPress.co.uk
online from www.LittleKnollBookshop.co.uk
and from UK bookshops

Printed in Great Britain by
Hobbs the Printers Ltd.
Totton, Hampshire

Avenger over HMS Indomitable

This book is dedicated to the memory of
Sub. Lt. (A) Geoffrey Eaton Wright RNVR
and all who served in 857 Squadron Fleet Air Arm.

857 Squadron, June 1944

i

CONTENTS

Part 2: The war in the Far East and the Pacific

Part 4: Sakishima Gunto: The 'unsinkable aircraft carriers'

PICTURE INDEX

FOREWORD

I have often heard people call the war in the Far East the 'Forgotten War.' Far from forgotten if you took part in it!

This book, so well researched, gives an absolute picture of the hazards and horrors which were suffered by those who were there.

The story of Sub. Lt. (A) G. E. Wright RNVR, which begins this book, tells of the complicated and thorough training of a Fleet Air Arm pilot. The essential amount of 'know how' required makes sense when one discovers the vast amount all pilots in this situation of extreme danger have to contend with.

The loss of life of those who fight on land, sea and in the air will increase the percentage of casualties when coupled with the dreadful and gruesome treatment the Japanese could inflict on captured prisoners, quite beyond normal comprehension.

I can recommend this book to those whose wish is to discover whether this 'Theatre of War' should be classed as 'Forgotten.'

Doug Gregory D.F.C.

Flight Lieutenant Doug Gregory D.F.C. joined the RAF at the age of 18 in 1941 and after his initial training sailed to Africa for his pilot training in Southern Rhodesia, gaining his wings in 1942. After returning to the UK he trained as a night fighter pilot, first flying Blenheims and then Beaufighters.

Flt. Lt. Gregory and his navigator flew to RNAS Gibraltar in early 1945 to fly different attack manoeuvres on the Fleet Destroyer HMS *Barfleur* to test the ship's radar systems prior to it joining the British Pacific Fleet in operations against the Japanese in the Pacific.

After the war Doug Gregory became an art teacher, until retirement at the age of 60. It was then he built his own replica of a First World War Royal Aircraft Factory S.E.5a over a period of four years. After it was built and had its first flight, he became part of the Great War Display Team that took part in displays at air shows all around England.

AUTHOR's PREFACE

It is often a deep interest in a particular area that stimulates a desire to research deeper and find out further information about a subject, and may lead to sharing your findings with others through writing a book. However, the spark of an idea for a project may come when you least expect it, and that is what happened to me with this book.

The daughter of an elderly gentleman was concerned that her father was not meeting many people and thought that if someone could visit him and spend time talking to him, then it would possibly cheer him up. I was approached by a friend who asked me if I could find the time to visit and have a chat with him, and that is how I came to meet Geoffrey Eaton Wright.

Geoffrey Eaton Wright
Courtesy of Richard De Jong

When I arrived for my first visit I was amazed at the large models of steam engines on display that Geoffrey Wright had made over the years. He told me about the hours he spent in making all the parts and creating the models.

On the walls there were a number of pictures, and from my interest in aviation I was attracted to a painting of a Grumman Avenger, with the caption underneath:

'Sub Lieutenant (A) RNVR Geoffrey E. Wright
857 Squadron 1944 (disbanded 1945)'

Further along the wall I saw a frame with a photograph of a very smart young man in uniform and asked Geoffrey if he was the young man in the photograph. He said he was, and pointed to the picture of the Grumman Avenger and said that was the aircraft he flew in the war.

I was intrigued by what I had seen and asked Geoffrey if he would like to tell me all about his time in the Fleet Air Arm in the Second World War. Apart from my deep interest in aviation and experience in oral history, where I have interviewed many people about their life's experiences, I also thought that it would give me the opportunity to visit Geoffrey more regularly and talk about his experiences as a pilot of an Avenger. So my association with Geoffrey Eaton Wright began.

From the start Geoffrey Wright was very complimentary about the quality of the flight training he received as part of the Towers Scheme in the USA from 1942-44, and how the constant checks on progress and intensity of practice, not just in training, but continued when on active service with the British Pacific Fleet, gave the pilots the skills to confidently engage the enemy in combat. However, this did not mean they were not nervous before going into combat, but as Geoff Wright commented, 'Once we went in everything seemed to be done on automatic.'

Geoffrey Wright talked about the lifelong friendships he had with fellow Fleet Air Arm pilots and mentioned a group of ex-pilots from 857 Squadron who had maintained contact and had met occasionally over the years, right up to the present time. However, he became very distressed when talking about the loss of many of his Fleet Air Arm colleagues while serving against the Imperial Japanese Forces, and especially when I informed him of the fate of his first American flying instructor, Lt. Vernon Tebo and his aircrew in the hands of the Japanese military.

The Forgotten Fleet

Geoffrey Eaton Wright's story gave me the challenge to research in depth the Royal Navy's involvement in the Far East with the Eastern Fleet, first based in Ceylon (now Sri Lanka) before being reorganised into the British East Indies Fleet, and finally the British Pacific Fleet, possibly the largest and most powerful fleet ever assembled by the Royal Navy.

After transferring to a new base in Sydney, Australia, the BPF became involved with US Forces Fifth Fleet in March, 1945 and designated as 'Task Force 57' for the attacks on the Sakishima Gunto (Islands) in support of the American landings on Okinawa, and later as 'Task Force 37' with the US Third Fleet for the final attacks on the Japanese homeland before its surrender.

The British Pacific Fleet and the East Indies Fleet became known as 'The Forgotten Fleet'. This was because following the celebrations for VE Day (Victory in Europe) in May, 1945, and VJ (Victory over Japan) Day in August, 1945, the British Pacific Fleet had long been forgotten when its ships and personnel arrived back, some well into 1946.

I feel very privileged to have been given the opportunity of meeting Geoffrey Eaton Wright to hear his personal story of the flight training he received in the USA and combat experiences as part of the British Pacific Fleet. In addition, to hear of the bravery and sacrifice of the many American, Australian, New Zealand, Dutch and British sailors and airmen, who had been subjected to the intense attacks by the Japanese aircraft, especially the deadly kamikaze aircraft, while maintaining the ongoing attacks with the American Task Units against the Sakishima Islands.

Sadly, Geoffrey Wright passed away not long after I had completed the interviews, but I know that he was very pleased to have the opportunity to share his wartime memories as a tribute to all the brave and courageous sailors and airman that he served with in the Pacific War.

Mike Roussel 2015

ACKNOWLEDGEMENTS

My special thanks to Doug Gregory D.F.C. for writing the Foreword to this book. Doug was a night-fighter pilot in the Second World War and went on to serve in India as a test pilot until his demob from the RAF in 1946. Sadly in 2015 Doug passed away and I would like to dedicate the Foreword to his memory.

It is also a great sadness that my friend Alan Mansell passed away while I was writing the book. Alan was a keen aviation photographer and was putting together a collection of photographs of Pacific War aircraft flying today, including the Corsair, Hellcat, Wildcat and Avenger, for my book. My grateful thanks go to Alan's wife, Lorraine, for sending me the photograph of the Corsair 130 A, which Alan took at Duxford and is displayed in this book.

I am indebted to Mrs Janice Rivett, daughter of Geoffrey Eaton Wright, for her help and support in accessing documentation and photographic evidence for my research, and also to his son-in-law, The Rev. Paul McVeagh, who was able to share some of the anecdotes that Geoffrey Wright had told him about his time with the 857 Squadron.

My grateful thanks go to all who have loaned me photographs from their collections. They include; Michael Pocock webmaster of www.maritimequest.com with photographs from the late Frank Stockwell, donated by his granddaughter Emma Stockwell, Ron Dupas of www.1000aircraftphotos.com with photographs from his own collection, including those by courtesy of Ray Crupi, Jacques Trempe, Bill Pippin, John Voss, and Joe Lawler, who also gave me additional information about his father, Keith Lawler Sr.

I am also indebted to Michael Nearing of www.ShipleyBay.com for his help and information on Lt. Tebo, and also to Kenneth M. Keisel and the Grosse Ile Historical Society.

My special thanks to Gordon Smith, www.naval-history.net for his support, and Paul Whiteing for allowing me to use photographs from his late father's collection. Maurice C. Whiteing was a leading air mechanic on the Fleet Aircraft Carrier HMS *Indomitable* in the Indian Ocean and Pacific Ocean from 1944-1945. HMS *Indomitable* was the Fleet Carrier that 857 Squadron Fleet Air Arm was based on.

I am particularly indebted to Richard McDonough of the Imperial War Museum sound archives for his help and support for my research, and to Mr Phil (Darby) Allen of the HMS St Vincent Association for his support and photographs of HMS St Vincent, Gosport.

Finally, I am eternally grateful to my wife Kay for her constant encouragement and support for my work and the patient acceptance of my daily disappearance for many hours into my study.

INTRODUCTION

The beginning of Military interest in Flight

In 1783 the first hot-air balloon was built and flown by the Montgolfier brothers in France, but by the time of the American Civil War, 1861-1865, both the Union and Confederate armies were using tethered balloons for reconnaissance. In 1862 two officers who had served with Thaddeus Lowe's Union Army Balloon Corps proposed the formation of a British Army balloon unit for aerial observation of enemy targets.

The School of Ballooning, known as 'the Balloon Factory' was based in the late 1800s in Aldershot, where it became one of the permanent units of the Royal Engineers. There had been experiments in the development of airships in 1902, and the first flight was undertaken by the British Army Dirigible No1 on the 10th September, 1907. It was named the *Nulli Secundus* and was flown by Colonel Capper and Samuel Franklin Cody.

Wilbur and Orville Wright's first powered flight at Kitty Hawk, North Carolina, USA, on the 17th December 1903, had influenced a massive interest in aviation development in the USA and also in Europe. Samuel Franklin Cody built the British Army Aeroplane No 1 at the Balloon Factory, and made the first British powered flight to 1,390ft (423.67m) in October 1908. Just one year later, Louis Blériot made the first crossing of the English Channel from France to Dover, and in the same year the US Army Signals Corps purchased their first aircraft, a Wright Model A, for its newly formed Aeronautical Section.

In 1911 the British Balloon Factory became known as the 'Army Aircraft Factory' and just one year later renamed the 'Royal Aircraft Factory'. The British interest in aircraft being used in warfare began with the formation of a Royal Engineers Air Battalion at Farnborough. The Air Battalion Royal Engineers had two areas: No 1 Company was equipped with Airships and based at Farnborough, and No 2 Company was equipped with aeroplanes

1

and based at Larkhill aerodrome, Salisbury Plain.

On 13th May 1912, the Royal Flying Corps (RFC) was formed, with the Central Flying School for training both army and navy pilots at Upavon, and with the Royal Aircraft Factory at Farnborough. In January 1914 the Royal Naval Air Service (RNAS) was formed. The main role of the RNAS was fleet reconnaissance and looking for enemy ships and submarines, but the RNAS also had squadrons on the Western Front. While the RNAS came under the control of the Admiralty, the RFC was under the control of the War Office.

Despite the huge developments in aviation in America during the first decade of the 20th century, there was a much slower start in its production and use of military aircraft, and in the build-up to the First World War it was the European countries that were to lead the way. Out in front were the French aircraft designers who began producing a range of aircraft for the French army to use in a military capacity.

At the start of the First World War aircraft were used first for aerial spotting of targets for ground fire, but this soon led to air combat between fighter biplanes. When the RFC (Royal Flying Corps) was formed in 1914, there was one observation balloon squadron and four aircraft squadrons, but their effectiveness of informing the artillery on targets for the ground fire was less efficient until they started to use radio communication in 1915. The RFC aircraft also proved themselves in the First World War in the use of photographic reconnaissance and observation, as well as fighters and bombers.

There was a range of aircraft flown by British Aces in the First World War, including Bristol Scouts, Sopwith Pups and Sopwith Camels, but by far the favourite was the Royal Aircraft Factory S.E.5a, which came into operation from 1917 and was used to great effect by the top aces, including Billy Bishop, Mick Mannock, James McCudden, Albert Ball, Andrew Beauchamp-Proctor, George McIlroy and Frederick McCall.

When the United States entered the First World War in 1917, the main US combat aircraft flown by the United States Air Service was built in America by the Curtiss Aeroplane Company, but a majority of their fighter planes were designed and built by the French and British, and included the French Niéuport and SPAD, along the British Sopwith Camel and Bristol F.2B.

In the 1920s it was not easy for the US Military to gain funding from the U. S. Government, but this came through the support the government gave to US aircraft manufacturers. The aim was to encourage the designing and development of high-performance aircraft that would compete in air races in America, including the Pulitzer Trophy Races for land planes and also international competitions such as the Schneider Trophy Contests for float planes. The US Army and US Navy air services used this opportunity to gain publicity and public support for extra funding from Congress. The racing aircraft were often flown by serving officers, which created an intense rivalry between the Army and Navy aviators for their service to win and be the best.

The world economic crises of the 1930s led to the Japanese military taking over governmental control in Japan, when they started to seize large areas of Chinese territory and began building up the Imperial Japanese Army and Navy. At the time, the Western Governments gave little attention to supporting China, but when the second Sino-Japanese war broke out in 1937 with China and the brutal treatment of Chinese civilians by the Japanese troops, it quickly led to a deterioration in the relationship between the United States and Japan.

In the early 1930s, Japanese Army and Navy air forces were poorly equipped with mainly aircraft designed and built by other countries. While in the build up to the Second World War the focus of attention had been on the Allies development of high-performance, heavily-armed fighters, the Japanese aircraft industry had been secretly engaged in designing and building aircraft that were lightweight, highly manoeuvrable and would be a formidable challenge to the Allies fighters in the Second World War. The Japanese pilots, who were also highly trained, were able to extend their combat experience in the second Sino-Japanese war from 1937, and were well prepared for a war in the Pacific.

When the Second World War started in 1939, the Imperial Japanese Army was very large, well equipped, well trained and was poised to expand the Japanese Empire even further into the Pacific and Southeast Asia. The Imperial Japanese Navy was at the time the largest and most powerful navy in the Pacific, and their approach to the use of aircraft carriers in a future war was well advanced.

The United States decided to remain neutral at the start of the Second World War, but remained in the background supporting the Allies with much needed food and supplies. That was until the Japanese attacked Pearl Harbour on the 7th December, 1941, causing the USA to declare war on Japan. A few days later the Germans and Italians declared war on the USA, bringing it fully into the Second World War.

This book starts with the story, through the eyes of a British Fleet Air Arm pilot, of his flight training in the USA with US Navy instructors before transferring to the newly formed 857 Avenger Squadron. After completing their United States training, 857 Squadron returned on HMS *Rajah*, a new build of escort carrier, along with their Avenger aircraft for their final training in Britain. The next stage was for the squadron to sail from Belfast on HMS *Rajah* to Ceylon (Sri Lanka) to join the newly formed British Pacific Fleet, and describes the strikes made on the Japanese military while transferring to a new base in Sydney, Australia.

As part of Task Force 57 the British Pacific Fleet joins the American fleet to launch attacks on the Sakishima Gunto (Islands) in support of the American invasion of Okinawa. The story describes the continuous attacks to crater the runways and destroy control and accommodation buildings on the Japanese airfields. The attacks were aimed at disrupting the transfer of newly built aircraft to Formosa and the kamikaze aircraft flying from Formosa to attack the American Fleet and British Pacific Fleet involved in the attacks on the Sakishima Islands and the American forces invasion of Okinawa.

Part 1: Training of Pilots for the Royal Navy Fleet Air Arm

CHAPTER 1

The development of Aircraft Carriers

In 1910 flight decks were introduced, after experimental decks were tried on the foredeck of warships, with the first fixed-wing take off from USS *Birmingham*. Other uses of aircraft were being developed with the seaplane carriers, the first being the French *La Foundre* in 1911 with a short deck for take-off with the aircraft lifted back on board by a crane. The first launch off a moving warship was from HMS *Hibernia* in May 1912. At the start of the First World War, the Imperial Japanese Navy were quick to develop their first aircraft carrier *Wakamiya,* and in September 1914 its Farman seaplanes were involved in the first naval aircraft air raid when they attacked the Austro-Hungarian cruiser *Kaiserin Elisabeth* and German gunboat *Jaguar* with bombs in Qiaozhou Bay, China. Although it was the first air-sea battle, the Japanese seaplanes did not manage to hit their targets.

The First World War gave the opportunity to develop the role of aircraft in combat, both at sea and on land. The use of land-based aircraft was introduced, first for target spotting, but soon in a combat role as a fighter over the battlefields in France. Taking off from a flight deck of a warship was successfully achieved for aircraft to undertake a reconnaissance role, but recovery was a problem and although the pilots could be saved from the water, often the aircraft was lost. It was not until 1917 when a pilot landed his Sopwith Pup on the flight deck of HMS *Furious* that the development of the flat top aircraft carrier for taking off and landing increased. HMS *Argus* was the first full length flat deck carrier to be able to launch and land naval aircraft in 1918.

The early flat top aircraft carriers were ships that had started life in a different role, such as cargo ships or other warships, but the first vessel designed and built as an aircraft carrier was the Imperial Japanese Navy *Hōshō*, built in 1922 and used in a test role for carrier operations.

It was during the 1920s that countries started to design and build aircraft carriers specifically for that role. The 1922 Washington Naval Treaty placed limits on the tonnage of warships, where the tonnage could not be exceeded for each vessel, and this led to some warships being converted into use as aircraft carriers. The first full-deck carrier for the United States was the USS *Langley* which was converted from another type of ship. The Royal Navy HMS *Hermes* of 1924 was built with a full-length flight deck, a starboard island and a hurricane bow. This was a bow that was sealed right up to the flight deck. Previous designs had open section bows which had guns for firing forward, but strong winds could get under the flight deck, especially when turning into the wind, and cause serious damage, but sealing that section avoided the problem, and it became the design for the future carriers. HMS *Hermes* served in World War II and eventually joined the Eastern Fleet in 1942, but was sunk by Japanese dive bombers off Trincomalee. A hospital ship that had witnessed the attack rescued most of the survivors.

There had been experiments by a number of countries during World War I and the intervening years before the Second World War in the use of submarine aircraft carriers. The Royal Navy had conducted experimental use of aircraft carrying submarines, using their M class submarines. HMS *M2* was used by replacing her 12 inch gun with a small hangar which housed a Parnell Peto floatplane. The aircraft would be catapulted off the deck of the submarine and after landing back on the water would be retrieved by a crane. The aircraft was used in a reconnaissance role, but HMS *M2* accidentally sank in Lyme Bay in 1932. It is thought that the hanger doors were opened too soon after surfacing and the submarine sank with all hands. After this loss the British withdrew from the use of aircraft carrying submarines. The Japanese however, did start using large submarine aircraft carriers, which were used extensively in World War II.

Aircraft carriers became very important in the Second World

War and the United States Navy, British Royal Navy and the Imperial Japanese Navy had been busy during the 1930s building large fleet carriers for their fleet air protection and also for attacks on enemy vessels or land bases. One innovation by the Royal Navy was the decision to use the armoured flight decks to protect the hanger deck where the aircraft were stored. This proved to be a good decision, especially in the Pacific War as a strong protective defence against the Japanese kamikaze aircraft crashing onto the flights decks. The American aircraft carriers, which were built with wooden flight decks, lost many of their carriers from kamikaze attacks. This was when the aircraft and bombs went through the wooden decks causing massive damage and fire on the inside of the carriers. Those carriers that were not sunk would then spend as much as six months in dry docks being repaired before they could return to active service.

In the USA the classification for the aircraft carrier was (CV) and at the beginning of World War II different types of carriers were introduced, including the escort carriers which were only used during the war, and had the new classification CVE (aircraft carrier escort). The escort carriers were much smaller than the fleet carriers and could carry a larger number of aircraft than the other types of carriers, and often were originally merchant ships converted for the period of the war. They were known affectionately in the US Navy as 'Jeep carriers' or 'Baby flattops' and in the Royal Navy as 'Woolworth carriers' because of their size in relationship with the large Fleet carriers. Some escort carriers were specifically built in US yards, and these included the US light aircraft carrier which was converted from the Cleveland-Class cruiser which was a much faster vessel. Until 1943 these carriers still had the classification CV, but it was then changed to CVL (aircraft carrier light).

Many of the escort carriers came under the American Lend-Lease agreement with the USA and were transferred to the Royal Navy. The first in 1941 was the Long Island Class escort carriers, which was just a two ship class of converted merchant vessels and consisted of the USS *Long Island* serving with the US Navy and the British HMS *Archer* (D78) serving with the Royal Navy. Their original classification was AVG (Aircraft Escort Vessels).

Another group of AVGs with a similar design were the four vessels in the Avenger class, HMS *Avenger, Biter, Dasher* and *Charger*. However, HMS *Charger* was returned to the US Navy service as USS *Charger* (CVE 30) in 1942 and became a carrier training ship for the pilots and crews. She was moored in Chesapeake Bay, USA, for the duration of the war. The Royal Navy ships were classified as BAVG's and of the remaining three Royal Navy ships, only the HMS *Biter* survived the war. All three escort carriers were involved in Operation Torch, the invasion of North Africa, but although HMS *Avenger* had taken part in the Russian Convoys and then Operation Torch, it was on 15th November 1942 that she was sunk by a torpedo from *U-155*. HMS *Dasher* continued after Operation Torch with ferry operations in the Mediterranean. While in the Clyde after returning with engine trouble she suffered a massive internal explosion on the 27th March 1943 and sank. The actual cause of the explosion remains a mystery. After the war USS *Charger* was refitted and renamed MV *Fairsea* and became a well-known post-war passenger ship.

The British had developed the large MAC ships, which were merchant ships developed from hulls of the Empire class grain carriers and tankers that had been fitted with a flat deck with an island. The small number of aircraft stored on deck was there to protect the convoys while on the transatlantic crossing.

There were also the CAM ships, that were other merchant vessels which had been fitted with catapults to launch their aircraft. CAM ships were only in existence for a short time on the transatlantic and arctic convoys, providing air cover until more escort carriers were available. The downside of this system was that no aircraft recovery was available and the pilot either had to make for the nearest land or ditch in the sea. Although there were some pilot losses, most were picked up from the water by a convoy vessel.

HMS *Audacity* (D10) was the first Royal Navy escort carrier that came into service in June 1941. She was originally the German Merchant vessel MV *Hannover* which was captured in March 1940. After two further name changes, first *Sinbad* and then

Empire Audacity, she was put into Blyth Dry Docks to be rebuilt as the first Royal Navy escort aircraft carrier. In her period of working up on the Clyde, 802 Naval Air Squadron started to land their Grumman Martlets on the flight deck. The design as an escort carrier had not included space for a lift and hanger deck and its six Grumman Martlets (Wildcats) were all stored on the flight deck.

Empire Audacity was renamed for the last time in July 1941when she became HMS *Audacity* and proceeded to support the Gibraltar convoys against the long range Fw 200 Condor reconnaissance/bombers.

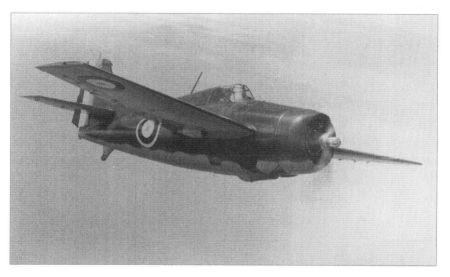

Grumman G-36A Martlet (Wildcat) Royal Navy. Delivered to RN Fleet Air Arm 1940. The first US Navy fighter with retractable landing gear.   Ron Dupas

HMS *Audacity* sailed with OG74 convoy to Gibraltar. That was when Sub. Lt. Eric 'Winkle' Brown shot down his first Fw 200 Condor, and on the return convoy HG 74 from Gibraltar one more Fw 200 Condor was shot down.

On the OG76 convoy to Gibraltar in October 1941, four Condors were shot down, one by Sub. Lt. Eric Brown, but there was the loss of one Martlet flown by the Commanding Officer Lt. Cdr. J. M. Wintor. When HG76 sailed from Gibraltar on the 14th December, 802 Squadron only had four of their Martlets that were in serviceable order, but the squadron still shot down two more Fw 200 Condors on that return voyage to the UK.

The operational experience of HMS *Audacity* found that a carrier could sail within the convoy and there it would have the protection of the other escort vessels. However, this limited the turning space needed when turning into the wind for the aircraft operations. HMS *Audacity* was to take the risk of sailing outside the convoy, but this gave the German U-boats a better opportunity of targeting her, and this was to be her fate.

HMS *Audacity* was leaving the convoy on the night of the 21st December 1941, while off Portugal, but a flare was let off from one of the convoy vessels which illuminated the shape of the escort carrier and gave the U-boats a clear target. She was identified by *U-751* (Gerhard Bigalk) who fired three torpedoes. The first torpedo hit the engine room and a further two torpedoes caused explosions which eventually sank HMS *Audacity*. There was a heavy loss of life, but Sub. Lt. Eric Brown, aged 22, was one of two 802 Squadron pilots to survive. Following the sinking of HMS *Audacity*, 802 Squadron was disbanded and not reformed until February 1942. Sub. Lt. Brown was then posted to the RAE (Royal Aircraft Establishment), Farnborough.

Types of Escort Carriers in the Second World War

The Sangamon Class, USS *Sangamon, Suwannee, Chenango* and *Santee*, were all converted oilers. Of all the US CVEs, these were very effective in the combat role and had large flight decks and hangers, but still retained their capacity to carry oil and were still able to act as oilers. In 1942 they took part in Operation Torch and also served in the Pacific War.

The Bogue class was a large group of escort carriers that were built in the USA for the US Navy and under the terms of Lend-Lease for the Royal Navy. However, approximately 75% of the Brogue Class were escort carriers used by the Royal Navy and renamed into two classes, the Attacker Class (1st Group) and the Ruler Class (2nd Group). Before delivery the ships needed modification to conform to the requirements of the Royal Navy and some of this work was undertaken in Vancouver, Canada. A number of Fleet Air Arm squadrons formed in the USA joined these newly built escort vessels, which then ferried the squadrons and their aircraft transatlantic to the UK.

There were escort carrier conversions carried out by the Royal Navy, including the three ships of the Nairana Class, HMS *Nairana, Vindex* and *Campania*. Two others were HMS *Pretoria Castle*, which remained as a trials and training carrier, and HMS *Activity*, that served on the transatlantic and Arctic before becoming a ferry carrier to the Far East 1944.

The largest group of escort carriers to be built by the United States was the Casablanca Class, and they remained in US Navy service. The intention was to transfer 50% of the Casablanca Class under the Lend-Lease terms to the Royal Navy, but instead the second group of Bogue escort carriers were sent as the Ruler class. However, quite a number of the Casablanca class were to work alongside the British Pacific Fleet in the Pacific War

The escort carriers of the British Pacific Fleet carried out replenishment and ferry duties to keep the large Fleet carriers supplied with aircraft and crews while involved in their combat duties in the Pacific War in 1945.

These included:

Attacker Class:	HMS *Striker* (D12)
	HMS *Chaser* (D32)
	HMS *Fencer* (D64)
Ruler Class:	HMS *Ruler* (D32)
	HMS *Arbiter* (D31)
	HMS *Slinger* (D26)
	HMS *Speaker* (D90)
	HMS *Reaper* (D82)
Nairana Class:	HMS *Vindex* (D15)

With the development of aircraft carriers came the planning for the training of future Fleet Air Arm pilots who would be taking off and landing aircraft on aircraft carriers. By the Second World War recruits for the Fleet Air Arm were given an early assessment for their suitability for learning to fly, and if successful trainees then received primary, intermediate and advanced training at land-based airfields, leading to specific training in ADDLs (Aerodrome Dummy Deck Landings) and finally to practice landings on aircraft carrier flight decks. This was high quality training that was to prove invaluable when pilots eventually went into combat.

Some training was undertaken in the UK, although many pilots trained in the USA and Canada.

CHAPTER 2

Pilot Training

The training of pilots for service in World War I was introduced, and many of the young pilots just out of training were sent to the battlegrounds in France, but many were quickly shot down by the more experienced German pilots. There was a need to ensure that the future combat pilots received training that gave them enough skill to survive long enough to gain effective combat experience and maybe eventually become flying aces.

By 1916, combat training started to be given to newly qualified pilots by pilots that already had gained combat experience in air battles, and in 1917 there was a joint agreement between America, Canada and Great Britain to work together in the training of pilots.

This first started in Canada, at Camp Borden, Ontario, and was followed by other flying training camps in Texas, USA. The RFC also had training camps in Egypt and there was an increase in volunteers to become pilots in the RFC from the British Empire, including Australia, South Africa and Canada, to fight in the First World War. In April 1918, the Royal Naval Air Service (RNAS) merged with the Royal Flying Corps (RFC) to form the Royal Air Force (RAF).

During the interwar period the RAF decided that there was a need to update and replace their front-line biplane fighters with the newer, well-designed, high-performance monoplane wing fighters. However, by the start of the Second World War in September 1939, the RAF realised they did not have enough fully trained pilots to fly them and started a training programme in the UK.

They soon ran into the problem of a shortage of flying instructors, due to the need for trained pilots in the operational squadrons. A further problem was the need to ensure that there were enough available operational bases in the United Kingdom for the fighters and bombers in the defence of Britain, and this did not help in finding enough airfields to operate pilot training. There was also the threat of airfields being bombed by German bombers, which would cause further delay to operational flights as well as the training of pilots.

The Germans engaged in building an Air Force of fast, deadly fighters for quite some time, and many of the Luftwaffe pilots had already gained valuable combat experience flying as part of the Luftwaffe Condor Legion in the Spanish Civil War from 1936-39.

With the closeness of the European continent to the UK the German Luftwaffe would not hesitate to attack and shoot down the inexperienced trainee pilots over the training airfields. What the RAF needed was airfields to train pilots and their aircrews that were far away from the battlefields of Europe.

British Commonwealth Air Training Plan

In December 1939 the British Government made an agreement with its dominions, Australia, New Zealand and Canada for the training of RAF pilots and air crew in Canada where there was better average weather conditions than in the UK and much larger open spaces for flight and navigation training. This was known as the (BCATP) British Commonwealth Air Training Plan, also known as the Empire Air Training Scheme in Australia and New Zealand, and established during the Second World War. Other training was undertaken in South Africa by the South African Air Force, and also in Southern Rhodesia as part of the Empire Air Training Scheme.

Arnold Flying Training Scheme

The Arnold Flying Training Scheme was set up in June 1941 after successful negotiations with the USA. This was for RAF cadets to be sent to the USA for flight training alongside USAAF trainees, and lasted to March 1943. The training consisted of three flying stages, with training taking place in separate primary, basic and advanced flying schools. The primary flying courses took place at flying schools in South Carolina, Georgia, Florida and Alabama.

Before travelling to North America for training, potential RAF trainees were given up to four hours on Tiger Moths. This was aimed at eliminating those who were unsuitable for pilot training for various reasons, such as suffering from air sickness, poor coordination or even those who found that their early experience was not what they expected and just did not like flying.

Once the pilot cadets arrived at Halifax on their requisitioned ocean liner, they travelled by train to Toronto, and then on to their primary flying school in the USA for their pilot training. After completing their flight training it was a train journey back to Halifax, Nova Scotia, and then a return transatlantic crossing to the UK.

The Towers Scheme

The Towers Scheme was promoted in 1941 by the US Navy's senior aviator, Rear Admiral John H. Towers, to train Royal Navy Fleet Air Arm pilots with USN instructors in the United States. He was also responsible for ensuring that the RN trainees were given access to the most up-to-date and best training aircraft. The training given to British trainees in the Towers Scheme was held in high regard by the Fleet Air Arm, and enabled the pilots to learn to fly the American built aircraft that they were to bring back to the UK as part of the Lend-Lease arrangements. The quality of the training and aircraft proved itself when in combat against the German Luftwaffe in Europe and against the Japanese pilots the Pacific War.

The Fleet Air Arm 'Y' (Youth) Scheme

The Fleet Air Arm of the RAF was formed in April 1924, to included fighters, reconnaissance aircraft and the torpedo bombers that were based on aircraft carriers, but was eventually returned to Admiralty control in May 1939. In order to attract potential pilots for the service, the RAF formed the Air Training Corps (ATC) for young boys still at school. The ATC also became a good attraction for recruits for the Fleet Air Arm.

In 1941, the Admiralty formed the Fleet Air Arm 'Y' Scheme

that was aimed to attract recruits from school who had received a good education and had the potential to become future officers. The requirement for acceptance on the 'Y' Scheme was a School Certificate and/or a recommendation from their headmaster.

Quite a few keen young men who were still at school were attracted to become Fleet Air Arm pilots through the 'Y' (Youth) Scheme. Posters had been distributed to schools explaining the Fleet Air Arm 'Y' Scheme. Those who were interested were interviewed and, if they were considered suitable, had a medical and then advised that they should join an organisation such as the ATC until they were called up at the age of 18.

Many young men chose to join the ATC while at school, and for those that had already left school and were engaged in work, there was always the Home Guard, where they had the opportunity to learn Morse code, or gain experience in marksmanship using the 0.303 Lee-Enfield rifles, and other military skills.

There was a determination among a lot of young men to serve their country and they chose service with the Army, Royal Navy or Royal Air Force. One young volunteer, who was to become a future pilot colleague of Geoffrey Eaton Wright in 857 Squadron, was Frank Stovin-Bradford. He was at the time studying architecture, but at the age of 17½ decided to apply for pilot training under the Fleet Air Arm 'Y' Scheme. After an interview and medical, which he passed, there was the 'waiting to be called up' when he reached 18 years of age. During this time he continued in the Home Guard and was called up in 1942 and reported to HMS Daedalus, Lee-on-Solent, as a Naval Airman Second Class.

Royal Naval Air Station Lee-on-Solent (HMS Daedalus)

A letter would arrive for the recruits who had applied to train as naval airmen on the Fleet Air Arm 'Y' Scheme, instructing them to report to HMS Daedalus, Lee-on-Solent, on a certain date. This would be the day that the new intake would arrive at HMS Daedalus to start their basic training.

Once all the new recruits had arrived in their civilian clothes and been allotted their accommodation, arrangements would first be made for them to collect their bedding, and then eventually they would collect their naval clothes and equipment and be measured for their uniform.

HMS Daedalus was known as a 'stone frigate' as it was a shore base, and the accommodation was a basic Nissen hut that had been originally designed in the First World War by a Canadian engineer Lt. Col. Peter Nissen. Nissen huts were also used extensively in the Second World War to accommodate soldiers, sailors and airmen at shore bases in the UK.

The Nissen huts were made of corrugated sheets bolted together to construct a semicircular arching roof and fixed to a concrete floor. The heating of the hut was mainly from a coke stove, either in the centre or towards one end of the hut. Inside were the double bunks, which were often bolted to the floor. It was the responsibility of the recruits to ensure that their accommodation was kept spotless and their beds made up for the daily inspection by the Petty Officer. The ablutions area and urinals would also be kept spotless by the recruits, and for some using a mop to wash the floor and a squeegee to push the water off would also be very new to them. Much of what they were learning was the same as if they were on board a naval ship.

The other important matter, after being allocated their accommodation, was to find the cookhouse and dining hall. There was the queuing for food, which was for some was better and more substantial than they could get at home, but if they were still hungry there was always the opportunity to go around again (around the buoy) and get another meal. If they were hungry at other times, they could always use the stove in the hut to cook some 'bacon butties', as long as they cleaned up well afterwards.

For many recruits having to become self-sufficient and ensuring that they kept themselves clean and well turned out was very new to them. This was especially found in washing clothes and laundry, which in the armed forces is known as the 'dhobi'. Then there is the ironing, labelling of clothes and darning holes in socks, something that their mother always did!

The day would start at 06.30 hours when a Petty Officer would come into the hut and rattle a stick against the side of the iron beds and shout at the men in the hut: 'Wakey, wakey, rise and shine, the sun's a burning your eyes out.' For the men in the hut it was pitch black because of the blackout on the windows, but outside the weather could be very different, and they soon found out if the Petty Officers wake-up call was correct. It was important to get out of bed quickly so they could be the first in the queue to wash and shave, often in cold water, and get back to dress and make their bed before the Petty Officer's hut and bed inspections by 7am.

Much of the training at HMS Daedalus was drill with plenty of 'square bashing', developing camaraderie and teamwork that grew during the training period. There was the seamanship, including tying knots, boatmanship and elementary navigation, but very little to do with being a naval airman and flying, apart from some aircraft recognition. During this early basic training anyone failing to come up to scratch was sent home. There were a number of famous people who passed through HMS Daedalus during the war and they included two famous actors, Lord Olivier and Sir Ralph Richardson, who also served as pilots in the Fleet Air Arm.

It was the instructors' aim to bring everyone to the same level, with little regard for social background, and to get the recruits to start to think as a team, After a month of basic training with drill and field-training, the recruits then moved to HMS St Vincent, Gosport, for the next part of their training, which was to focus more on them becoming naval airmen.

CHAPTER 3

Joining the Royal Navy in the Second World War

Geoffrey Eaton Wright was to be a future officer pilot in the Fleet Air Arm, but his route was to be different to many other recruits who had joined the Fleet Air Arm 'Y' Scheme. Wright had volunteered for the Royal Navy because he wanted to eventually join friends who were on the Royal Navy Fast Torpedo Boats, but this was not to happen, because his Divisional Officer decided to send him for a Fleet Air Arm interview.

Geoffrey Wright was born on the 26th April 1923 to the Reverend Robert and Kitty Wright, in Stoke Newington, London, where his father was a curate in a poor area of the city. They then moved to Kilburn, where his father became vicar, then to Mayfair, and finally Osterley.

The family moved to Osterley on the Great West Road where Wright's father, Dr Robert Frances Wright, became vicar of St Mary's, Osterley, and would preach once a year in St Paul's Cathedral. Geoffrey Wright's education started at Harrow View School, followed by St Paul's Public School, Hammersmith, where he took up rowing as one of his interests.

In 1939, when Wright was aged 16, the war broke out. While still at St Paul's School he became a dispatch rider for the ARP (Air Raid Precautions) at weekends, and later progressed to the Prime Minister's dispatch messenger service. He also joined the Army Cadet Force and remembers going on twenty mile route marches at night, carrying a backpack. It was assumed at the time that he was officer material, but Wright was not too keen on joining the Army. At the age of 18 he attended Selwyn College, Cambridge, following in the footsteps of his father who had also studied there. The day after arriving at Cambridge, Wright went to the Naval Recruitment Office and signed on, but was told that he could stay at University until he was half-way through his university course.

After St Paul's School had been evacuated, and for the remainder of the war, the original London buildings of the school in Hammersmith became the base for the XXI Army Group, under the command of General Bernard Montgomery (later Field Marshal), who also had been a pupil at St Paul's School. It was there that the military planning for the D-Day landings in June 1944 took place.

Training as an Ordinary Seaman at HMS Ganges

Geoffrey Wright was called up in June 1942 and sent to HMS Ganges, Ipswich, for training as an ordinary seaman, which he did not enjoy at all. Until the outbreak of the Second World War, HMS Ganges had been used as a boys' training establishment, but this was changed for the period of hostilities to the training of ordinary seamen.

Ordinary Seaman Wright GW Collection

The new recruits were first instructed on the routines and procedures of HMS Ganges, and then it was down to haircuts, kit issue, including bell bottoms and tops, finding their living accommodation and bunks, ablution facilities, which they had to keep spotless, as well as their kit. They had to ensure their own personal hygiene, often washing and showering in cold water, and also dealing with their dhobi (washing) and ironing. It was a tough regime, but the parade drills, sports, PE, including boxing, aimed to develop comradeship and teamwork, built the trainee recruits into learning naval discipline and life. However, it was not quite so easy for Wright and three other recruits when the Petty Officer in charge made them leading hands. Along with another student from Cambridge and two older men, they were selected to take charge of the sixty recruits, and wore a blue band with a red cross on their arms to distinguish them from the recruits. They were not very popular with the recruits they were in charge of, as they were instructed not to do any of the work, but to make sure the recruits did it.

Wright explains how this came about:

'We were all cleaning up the Officers' Mess. The Petty Officer in charge of us came in and gathered the four of us who were leading hands, and said, 'No, No, No! You mustn't do any of the work. Your job is to make sure the recruits obey orders.'

Of course the recruits heard what he said and hated us for that and took every opportunity to remind us by saying, 'You wait till we get to Chatham, we are going to kill you there.'

I found it a horrible time, but some good came out of it, because at the end of the course I was awarded a silver bosun's whistle.'

While at HMS Ganges, the Divisional Officer suggested that Wright joined the Fleet Air Arm as a pilot. He was not too keen on that, because he wanted to join his friends who were on the MTBs (Motor Torpedo Boats). The officer took no notice of his reply and issued him immediately with a train pass and sent him down to the West Country to be interviewed by a Naval Captain and three Royal Marine Commandos.

At the interview Wright was asked why he didn't want to join the Fleet Air Arm and he said, 'Well most of my friends have joined the Motor Torpedo Boats and that is what I want to do.'

He was firmly informed that he was going to be a pilot in the

FAA, although he was given an option which certainly made him change his mind:

'The Naval Captain told me that a ship had just returned for repairs after being attacked, and asked if I would prefer to be a navigator on the ship. I thought, blow that, I'd rather be a pilot, and told them that I had changed my mind and would now be willing to be considered for a position as a future naval pilot.'

Wright completed his training at HMS Ganges and then went to Portsmouth for a week, and then on to HMS Vincent, Gosport, the training establishment for naval airman.

HMS St Vincent, Gosport

New recruits would arrive at the main gate of HMS St Vincent having been warned in advance about the tough regime they would be entering in that establishment. Facing them through the gate was the parade ground surrounded by Victorian buildings, and opposite the main gate was the main mast from an 18th century warship, with an accommodation block behind. The mess and classrooms were on the ground floor and on the first and second floor were the dormitories and ablutions.

HMS St Vincent Main Gate.   Courtesy of HMS St Vincent Association

They would be greeted by the famous Chief Petty Officer Wilmot, who took them all under his 'wing and watchful eye', and would be keen to see they did plenty of drill, weapons training and seamanship.

Chief Petty Officer Wilmot had previously served on HMS *Nelson* as a naval gunner, in the post as chief gunner's mate. He was reputed to have been awarded the BEM after he had shot down a German aircraft with a Lewis machine gun from the roof of the accommodation block.

Portsmouth was a prime target for bombing by German aircraft, and after the sirens had sounded, C.P.O. Wilmot had ordered the cadets into the air-raid shelters, which had been built below the parade ground. He then climbed to the top of the accommodation block and prepared the Lewis gun with ammunition and saw all the bombs exploding over Portsmouth, and the flashes from the AA guns as they fired at the attacking aircraft.

A German Heinkel was heading towards HMS St Vincent, and C.P.O. Wilmot concentrated his fire at the aircraft, which was coming straight towards him. He could see the flashes of its guns firing at him, but kept his aim on the Heinkel, which flew over him and started to catch fire, gradually losing height and then crashing into the sea. A satisfied C.P.O. Wilmot then left the roof of the accommodation block.

Chief Petty Officer Wilmot has been described as quite a smallish man with 'yellow fangs' (his discoloured teeth), bloodshot eyes and a loud raucous voice, that has been described as 'like a rusty winch', which could be heard miles away. Despite his ferocious outward appearance, not all saw him that way and he has also been described as having a 'heart of gold.'

One recruit commented, 'He was lovely. We respected him and he respected us.'

It was well known that Chief Petty Officer Wilmot would greet each new course in a similar way. He would stand with his cap set on the back of his head and inform them of the programme of training that was to continue without a break throughout their time at HMS St Vincent, but adding that:

> '... left to their own devices, Naval airmen are quite happy to live in filth and squalor and it is our job to train you in more sanitary ways',

C.P.O. Wilmot. Courtesy of HMS St Vincent Association

C.P.O. Wilmot would then tell them he was not going to allow that and inform them of the daily dormitory and ablution cleaning, and room inspections, and explain the weekly block cleaning procedure. This was to start on the second floor of the accommodation block, with the cadets collecting buckets of water, pouring it on the dormitory floors and then brushing the water to the steps, where it then flowed down to the first floor. They then repeated the procedure until the block had been thoroughly cleaned to C.P.O. Wilmot's satisfaction.

Chief Petty Officer Wilmot's drill technique was to ask for 'them that have been to public school or have been in the ATC.' Those that put up their hands would then be chosen to drill the recruits, while he watched from a distance. The learning of skills in seamanship still went on, and for some their first experience in rowing a 20-oared whaler. However, for Wright there were no problems, because he had learned to row when he was a pupil at St Paul's Public School, Hammersmith. They learned to handle a machine gun, tie knots and the procedures of naval life. Although HMS St Vincent was a shore base, the terminology was still 'being on board', and when off duty the cadets went into Gosport or Portsmouth, they were 'going ashore'.

As the training was now focused on them becoming naval airmen they were known as 'officer cadets' and would have a white band on their hats, denoting 'officers in training'. After about eight weeks at HMS St Vincent, the cadets were examined in navigation, meteorology, Morse code, semaphore, seamanship and basic theory of flying, including aircraft recognition, and finally passed out as Acting Leading Naval Airman with an anchor on their sleeves.

Officer Cadets on Parade.   *Courtesy of HMS Vincent Association*

The next stage was to start their elementary flying training, and they were asked to choose where they would like to go for their continuing flight training.

There were the choices of starting their elementary flying training with the RAF at No 14 EFTS (Elementary Flight Training

School) at Elmden, Birmingham, and No 19 EFTS Sealand, in the Wirral, where they would fly de Havilland Tiger Moths, or to 24 EFTS Luton, where they were trained in a Miles Magister. From there, some would go to Canada for the next part of their flying training. However, many chose to go instead to the USA, where they would be taught by the United States Navy as part of the Towers Scheme.

Acting Leading Airman Wright was asked the question, 'Would you like to be taught by the American Navy or the Canadian Air Force?' His answer was that he would rather be taught by the American Navy as he felt that their pilots possibly had more combat experience than the Canadian Air Force pilots. It was then preparation for a transatlantic crossing to America where he was to undertake his training.

Fleet Air Arm training in North America

The US support to the Royal Navy's Fleet Air Arm involvement in World War Two was through the Lend-Lease aid programme to the British Empire. The US Senate passed the Lend-Lease Act on the 8th March 1941 and this gave the US President the authority to offer and extend aid to any countries who were contributing to the defence of the United States.

The Fleet Air Arm had an administrative base in Washington DC from October 1941, known as 'HMS Saker'. Many Fleet Air Arm Pilots received their training at US Navy Air Stations, including deck-landing training on USS *Charger* in Chesapeake Bay, Norfolk, Virginia, before returning to the UK with their American aircraft. The British Pacific Fleet saw service alongside the United States Navy in the Pacific and some Fleet Air Arm squadrons were actually attached to US aircraft carriers.

Transatlantic voyage to New York

The Fleet Air Arm trainee pilots were taken on the westbound transatlantic journey on ocean liners that had been requisitioned for the war effort. The ports they arrived at included New York, Boston, and Halifax, Nova Scotia, when they would be taken by train, first to their holding base in RCAF Moncton, Canada, and then by train to the US Navy Air Base for their primary training.

The eastbound transatlantic convoys were mainly bringing American troops over from the United States to be based in the UK to prepare for the invasion of Europe. As well as the troopships, there were the merchant ships that were bringing essential supplies of food, oil and war materials to Britain, sailing in convoys protected by escort destroyers from the German submarines that were lying in wait.

In April 1943, Acting Leading Airman Wright travelled to Liverpool to embark on the *Empress of Scotland* 26,313 GT. The *Empress of Scotland* was previously named the *Empress of Japan* 26,000 GT, which had been built for the Canadian Pacific Steamship Company trans-Pacific service. She was renamed after the Japanese attack on Pearl Harbour, but because wartime regulations prohibited the renaming of ships, it took about ten months to do so. It was the intervention of the Prime Minister, Winston Churchill, who thought having an allied ship with the name of an enemy country was absurd, and so the name was changed to *Empress of Scotland*.

The *Empress of Scotland* sailed from Liverpool on the 5th April 1943, arriving at New York on the 14th April 1943. Some of the airmen were not very good sailors and for those living below decks, the transatlantic crossing was not a very comfortable experience. However, there were those who volunteered to take on other duties, including jobs such as being an Oerlikon gunner, and were taught how to fire the cannon by the Merchant Navy. The advantage of taking these duties was that they were on the top deck and not stuck below decks, although they did meet up most days with their friends. A big plus was the 'jolly good food' they received during their time as volunteer gunners.

On some requisitioned liners, such as the '*Queens*', there were duties organised for 8 hours on/8 hours off, which included observation duties on deck. This was one of the ways to get around the increased numbers on board, who had to share accommodation with as many as twenty-two in a cabin, which would normally hold nine. The duties of 8 hours on and 8 hours off would then resolve that problem through the use of 'hot bedding', where one man gets out of bed to go on duty while another gets into the bed after being on duty.

Those travelling on the RMS *Queen Elizabeth* and RMS *Queen Mary*, and other ocean liners sailing into New York between February 1942 and September 1943, would have seen the capsized, burned out wreck of the French Line *Normandie* at Pier 88.

The French Line *Normandie* 79,280 GT was launched in 1932 and made her maiden voyage from Le Havre to New York on 29th May 1935. Due to the outbreak of the Second World War she arrived in New York on the 28th August 1939 and remained there until the United States entered the war after Pearl Harbour. She then taken over by the US Navy and renamed USS *Lafeyette*, and work started on converting her to a troopship. But on February 9th 1942, almost when her conversion was complete, a spark from a welder's torch set her on fire. She capsized onto her port side at Pier 88 and lay there in water until she sank, remaining in New York until refloated in September 1943, and eventually scrapped at Newark, New Jersey, in 1946.

Travel to Canadian Holding Base

The usual procedure for the naval airmen was to travel by rail to RCAF Monkton, New Brunswick, the holding base in Canada, before being sent to their training units. When they arrived at RCAF Moncton, they were housed in excellent accommodation with central heating and given food that they had not eaten for years. If they arrived at RCAF Moncton in the North American winter, they would be issued with cold weather gear and also be required to undertake guard duties. There was always the opportunity to play games against the other units on the camp and those who had learned to skate in the UK could always play ice hockey against the Canadians.

The next stage was to travel by rail from RCAF Monkton via Toronto to Grosse Ile, Detroit, Michigan. That journey took three days, while they slept in their seats and had their food brought to the carriages. It was then on to the USNAS (United States Naval Air Station) Grosse Ile, where they were to start their pilot training.

Long Railway Journeys.   *Geoffrey Wright*

CHAPTER 4

Flight Training at US Naval Air Station, Grosse Ile, Michigan, USA

Grosse Ile was officially commissioned on the 7th September 1929 as the Naval Reserve Air Base Grosse Ile, Detroit, Michigan. Its first adventure into aviation was the Aircraft Development Corporation of Detroit construction of an all metal airship, which was designated ZMC-2 (Zeppelin Metal Clad). This was the only airship ever built in the world with a metal skin. The metal used was duraluminium, a thin aluminium skin which was resistant to corrosion. ZMC-2 first flew on August 19th, 1929, at Grosse Ile, and then transferred to its permanent base at Lakehurst Naval Air Station, New Jersey, in October 1929, for use by the US Navy. After achieving 752 flights by 1936, its flying time was drastically reduced and the airship was eventually scrapped in 1941. ZMC-2 was photographed in a hanger alongside the German Zeppelin *Hindenberg* LZ 129 before the *Hindenberg* disaster took place when docking at Lakehurst on the 6th May 1937, with a large loss of life.

In August 1935 the base at Grosse Ile started training naval cadets, and by 1941 US Navy reserve squadrons were called up and the training of new cadets was increased, the same year as the first British students arrived. To accommodate the increasing number of cadets, new buildings were quickly constructed, including the barracks, classrooms, gymnasium, swimming pool, medical facilities and a link trainer room.

Grosse Ile was one of the first stations to receive British students, and by 1942 many of the British students would arrive from the Royal Navy Fleet Air Arm and be trained to fly in combat with the British Pacific Fleet alongside the US Navy against the Japanese. There were over 1,800 British students trained at Grosse Ile and some who lost their lives in training accidents are buried at the Oak Ridge Cemetery, Grosse Ile.

Development of the airfield

Grosse Ile airfield was a huge area of grass with three 150ft wide runways, built in a triangular pattern with a concrete central area for the aircraft to be parked. The name of the base was changed to US Naval Air Station, Grosse Ile, on December 9th 1942.

One of the aims of the US Naval Air Station, Grosse Ile, in the first weeks of the students arrival, was to single out those students who were considered suitable for training and reject those who were not. Grosse Ile was known as an 'E (Elimination) base' and the instructors were quite ruthless in this process. Those finally selected for training would eventually transfer to the US Naval Air Station, Pensacola, to continue with the next stage of their training.

Training Life for British Students

To Acting Leading Airman Wright the living conditions were very much like a boarding school, with highly polished floors and beds bolted to the floor and toilets without doors. This problem was quickly resolved when they discovered on visiting the canteen that its toilets had doors.

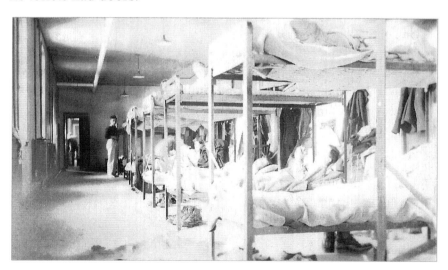

Dormitory Life   *Geoffrey Wright Collection*

The food was excellent, especially being able to eat an orange and all the other luxuries that he hadn't seen for a long time:

'In the morning the steward would come in at 7am and wake you up. Then it would be getting ready and down to the canteen, getting a tray, and line up where three or four chefs would dish up your breakfast.

At first it was a period of settling in where we were given ground instruction, and as well as learning about the aircraft and engines, there was classroom instruction where we received instruction in aerodynamics, meteorology, navigation, and knowing the clouds and which ones to avoid, including other important flight procedures for safety and organisation, before starting on our actual flight training.

There was continuous assessment weekly, which had to be passed. Those students who did not achieve the expected grades left the course, returned to New York, and then on to another transatlantic voyage back to the UK. It was quite a challenging time, with the American instructors giving us a tough time and making sure that we were up to the requirements for flying, and were ready to embark on the next stage of our flight training, which was taking to the air!

Our first task was to be kitted up for flying in an open cockpit. It did not matter if it were summertime; flying at 10,000ft would still be cold. We were issued with a helmet, goggles, fur jacket and boots, which we put over the top of our bellbottoms. Our first instruction would be showing us how to put on our flying kit before we went for our first flying lesson.'

The students would then be directed to the room where the mission blackboards were situated. These blackboards would inform the students the name of their instructor and who they would be flying with that day, or if with another instructor whose responsibility was to check on the student's progress. The blackboard would also indicate flight times and the training they would be undertaking that day. These blackboards were very important and the students were required to make sure they checked each day to see what they were going to do. Acting

32

Leading Airman Wright almost lost his place at Grosse Ile by not checking the board when due for his first solo flight, as will be seen later.

The first flights undertaken were with the flying instructor as pilot and the cadet as passenger in the rear cockpit. At each stage of his training the cadet pilot would first undertake familiarization of equipment, aircraft, take-off, landing and learning the local area they would be flying over. As training progressed the trainee would be shown and then practice various aerobatic manoeuvres, formation flying and night flying, including visual and radio instrumental navigation.

The first training aircraft the trainees were to use was the Spartan NP1, a two-seat primary trainer designed and built by the Spartan Aircraft Company for the United States Navy reserve units. This was considered by the trainees as a good plane for their initial training.

Spartan NP1

On the 10th July 1940 the Spartan Aircraft Company received an order from the United States Navy for 201 aircraft for use as a two-seat primary trainer biplane. This was an updated version of the company's 1927 C-3 open-cockpit biplane.

Spartan NP1 (3646) US Navy. This was the type of trainer that the future President of the United States, H.W. Bush, first flew solo at Grosse Ile.
Jacques Trempe Collection.

The NP1 was a conventional biplane, with two seats for pilot and student sitting in tandem open-cockpits, with fabric covered wings and fuselage. NP1 was 24ft 3ins (7.4m) in length and 8ft 4ins (2.54m) height, with a wingspan of 33ft 9ins (10.29m) and powered by a 220hp (164kW) Lycoming R-680-8 radial engine, giving cruising speed of 90 mph (145 km/h) and maximum speed of 108 mph (174 km/h), a range of 315 miles and a ceiling of 13,200ft (4025m). Its original designation by the company was NS-1, but the plane was given the military designation NP-1.

Primary Flight Training

Primary flight training is divided into six stages, starting with:

1. Primary Dual: with instructor, taxiing, take-off, landings, stalls, spins and primary emergency procedures - solo check flight.

2. Primary Solo: Review of dual instruction with more advanced tasks and techniques.

3. Advanced Solo: includes loops, Immelmann Turn, Split-S and 'Falling Leaf'.

4. Final: both dual instruction and solo demonstration, includes review with focus on smoothness of flying techniques and more advanced stalls and spins.

5. Formation Flying: three-plane V formation, echelon and landings in V.

6. Night Flying: Dual and solo night flying instruction.

Primary Dual is the first stage where the student flies with the instructor and learns the basics of flying, which will include taxiing to take-off and climb, leading turns, spirals glides and landings. The student will then be introduced to how to control stalls, spins and undertake emergency procedures. This will be concluded with the student going solo, which is checked by the instructor. At each stage the cadet will be checked before moving to the next stage.

Lt. Vernon Tebo, Flying Instructor, introduces Primary Dual Training

All trainee flying cadets were allocated a flying instructor, and fortunately for Acting Leading Airman Wright, he found his main flying instructor was Lt. Vernon Tebo. The American colleagues of Lt. Tebo saw him as a man who was 'quiet, religious, courteous and always considerate to others', which independently, 70 years later, Geoffrey Eaton Wright told the author, was the man he got to know.

Flight Training commenced and the first entry in his log book was on May 13th 1943 and reads, 'Flight familiarization'. This consisted of a talk by Lt. Tebo about the aircraft and its controls:

'Lt. Tebo came into the crew room when he was ready to take me up for my first flight. We then went out onto the apron, where there were many aircraft, and he introduced me to the first NP1, No 3754, that we would go up in. After walking around and explaining about the aircraft, we got on board with Lt. Tebo in the front and me sitting in the rear cockpit. The first thing was a cockpit check. Lt. Tebo started the engine, with a man at the front of the aircraft to swing the prop. I was surprised by the number of aircraft, which I estimated at about forty to fifty, taking off, landing and flying around the airfield at approximately 2,000ft. I wondered what the local residents may have thought about the noise of all the aircraft flying around!'

The Control Tower systems were rigid, and up to five aircraft could be landing at a time on the runway, as long as they had a green light. A red light would indicate flying around again, and these procedures had to be rigidly adhered to by the trainee pilots for the safety of all who were in the air or landing at the time.

'Once we were ready to leave the apron, Lt. Tebo then taxied for take-off, and once in the air, did a fly around of the local area while he gave me information through the intercom to familiarise me with the area I would be flying over and the position of the airfield for returning and landing.

I remember during my flights with Lt Tebo that he would often sing with an excellent singing voice through the microphone and I would join in as well. We sang many of the Glenn Miller tunes together, with Lt Tebo imitating the musical instruments and the rhythm of the tune. I also remember that Lt Tebo had written on the back of the band of his goggles 'RELAX! RELAX! RELAX!''

Each flying day, Lt. Tebo would come into the crew room and meet Wright and review what they had completed in the previous session, discussing what they would be doing that day. From May 13th to May 29th Lt Tebo was at the controls and demonstrated various important flying manoeuvres that included Turns and Stalling, Touch and Go Landings and Spins, S. Turns, Taxiing and Primary Emergencies:

'I remember one session when I went up with Lt. Tebo to the aerobatic area, which was a little way from the airfield, when he demonstrated various aerobatic manoeuvres. During my time with Lt. Tebo he gave me the nickname of 'Wilbur', after Wilbur Wright of Wilbur and Orville Wright fame. That nickname stayed with me throughout my time in the Fleet Air Arm.'

On May 29th, Lt. Tebo did a check of landings and spins, and the same day this was followed by another instructor, Ensign House, whose task was to assess his progress under the tuition of Lt. Tebo for the month. All entries in the log book were by the month and regular stage checks were made on his tuition and flying by other flying instructors.

The importance of learning these flying skills were for the trainee pilot to experience the different flight characteristics and problems, and learn how to control possible problems. Wright explains the processes that he practiced and learned:

'For the turns and stall, it is quite possible that on a turn you could stall the aircraft, especially on a steep turn, and the aircraft starts falling. You have to push the stick forward and gain speed. Depending on the spin direction, you put the rudder to the left or right to recover and then pull the stick back gently, start going up for a short while, and then straighten out. There were a lot of trainee pilots that were killed doing this manoeuvre.

For touch and go we would fly around the airfield and touch down on the runway and take off again. This would be repeated many times and it was the best way to teach you to do these manoeuvres properly.

One of the most important things in flying is coordination, and quite a few were failed because they lacked coordination in flying an aircraft. When we did the emergencies we were learning to recover from a spin. This could find the pilot freezing when trying to gain control in a spin, and for many, the instructors shouting to the trainee to 'LET GO!'

On June 5th 1943, Wright went solo for two flights, but he remembers that he almost got kicked out for failing to check the blackboard which informed him on when he was put down for solo: 'I forgot it and missed it and thought I would be kicked out.' Lt. Tebo said, 'Watch the blackboard, because it is there you will be told when you will first fly solo.'

The next day he was fortunate to have another chance and his name was on the board to fly solo for the first time. He remembers his first solo flight very well:

'I found it terrifying, because sitting in the backseat you have a very good view of the area you are flying in, but in the front cockpit the pilot's view of the ground was more restricted.

I took off and flew around the airfield and undertook two or three touch and go, and you can bet Lt. Tebo was watching me very carefully.

I was very relieved after I had landed that I had successfully completed my first solo flight. The same day I went up for my second solo flight, which I also completed successfully.'

Conversion to the N2S Trainer for Primary and Advanced Solo Training

Primary solo training started with a review of the dual instruction and then moved on to more advanced manoeuvres and skill, with the instructor giving dual instruction and student demonstrating what he had learned. These manoeuvres included steep turns and wingovers, spirals, slips and small fields, undertaken with both dual and solo demonstration.

On June 6th 1943 Wright transferred from the NP1 to undertake his next period of training on the N2S and was given his conversion instruction from Lt. Tebo.

The Stearman Aircraft Company primary trainer was designed in 1933 for the U.S. Army Air Corps, but the U.S. Navy became interested and ordered their first models in 1935, which was the NS-1, with the later versions known as the N2S, the model that Wright was to fly in. In 1939 Stearman became part of the Boeing Aircraft Company. The trainer was known by the US Army as the 'Kaydet' and by the US Navy as the 'Yellow Peril.'

The Boeing/Stearman Model 75 N2S was built as a two-seat primary trainer. It was 25ft (2.6m) in length and 9ft 2ins (1.79m) in body width. It had a wingspan of 32.2ft (9.80m) and was powered by a Lycoming R-680-17 radial with a cruising speed of 106mph (171km/h) and maximum speed of 124 mph (200 kp/h), a range of 505mph (813km) and a ceiling of 11,200ft (3315m).

Stearman N2S 07928   *Ray Crupi Collection*

Surviving N2S Trainers

Stearman N2S Trainer 42-07131   Courtesy of Bob Brockmann

After the war many of these aircraft were sold and became crop-dusters, but also a number survive today in private hands. Today Bob Brockman of Cochran, Georgia, owns Stearman 42-07131, which he bought from his brother and has been in his family since 1973. The Stearman is now based in Cochran, Georgia. Bob Brockman knows that the aircraft was stationed at Olathe, Kansas, and at Grosse Ile. It was at Grosse Ile that Bob Brockman first flew solo, and he says, 'I received my flying licence while flying from Grosse Ile, but at that time I had never heard of a Stearman.'

During his flight training Wright was to fly the N2S-1, N2S-2, N2S-3 and N2S-4. On checking his logbook for the N2S Stearman he flew, although it appears he did not fly 07131, he did fly 07153 and 07160 in June 1943.

Practicing Flying Manoeuvres

By June 8th, Wright was undertaking steep turns and wingovers and went solo the same day. A wingover is a flight manoeuvre when the pilot pulls the aircraft up into a steep climb until the aircraft almost stalls and then allowing the nose of the aircraft to fall away, turns until pulling out of the dive and then continues normal flight in the opposite direction.

Wright explained how he enjoyed practicing the steep turns and wingovers:

> 'For the steep turns and wingovers you go up almost vertically, kick the rudder either left or right when you turn slowly and then come down at speed. It was all very exhilarating!'

For the rest of June, Wright was given instruction on various manoeuvres by Lt. Tebo, and then plenty of practice of what he had been shown while flying solo. One of the procedures was 'slips and small fields' when he was required to learn how to come in and land on small fields:

> 'That was practicing landing on a field you haven't been to before. It could be an emergency where you have engine problems or are short of fuel.'

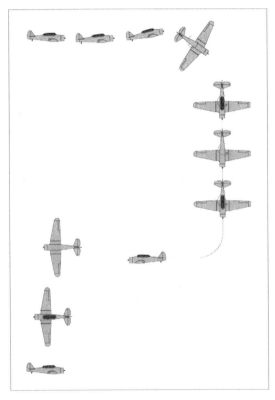

Spins   *Illustration by Dave Hatchard*

During this part of Wright's training he was taken by the instructors into the Advanced Solo, that included a combination of dual instruction and solo demonstration where the student would engage in Loops, Immelmann turns, Split-S and the 'Falling Leaf'.

The 'Falling Leaf' was very similar to watching a leaf falling through the air when it goes from side to side until in lands on the ground. Wright explains this procedure:

> 'You go slow and pull the stick back and stall the aircraft one way, correct by pushing the rudder the other way and then do the same the other way and this will be similar to the falling leaf.'

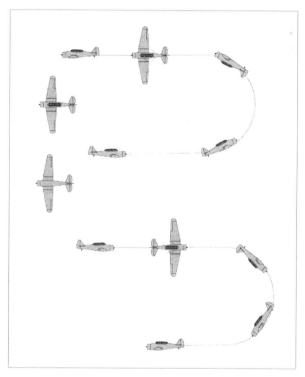

Top: Immelmann Turn   Bottom: Split-S
Illustrated by Dave Hatchard

As well as the falling leaf, Wright was shown how to undertake the Immelmann turn. This manoeuvre is named after the German WWI fighter ace, Max Immelmann, and is an aerobatic version of

41

the attack manoeuvres he used during dogfights in the First World War.

The manoeuvre is to fly in a straight level course and then enter a loop, climb vertically on full power and complete, then loop at the top with the aircraft then flying upside down. At the top of the turn straighten out into level flight while on the aircraft is still on its back, and then roll through 180° till the aircraft is again level and the correct way up, while continuing in level flight going in the opposite direction, but at a higher altitude.

The Split-S is a similar manoeuvre to the Immelmann turn, but basically reversing the procedure. The aircraft is in a straight and level flight at a higher altitude, and then rolls 180° onto its back and into a dive towards the ground, pulling out of the dive and into straight and level flight going in the opposite direction and at a lower altitude, but again the correct way up.

The final of dual and solo work found the student engaged in increased practice on reviewing what had been learned, and found Wright taking off and flying solo for reviews for some five to six times in a day.

The final Two Stages-Formation Flying and Night Flying

From July 1st to 16th Wright continued his flying with Lt. Tebo when other manoeuvres were practiced. These included inverted spins, night flying, strange field procedure, formation flying and a solo flying check.

On July 17th Wright changed back to flying the NP1, first with initial instruction by Lt. Tebo on V formation take-off, turns and breakaway. His next flight that day was with Lt. Umphras for a solo formation check.

The next day, July 18th it was down to Wright flying solo twice and practicing the manoeuvres he had had demonstrated to him by the instructors. On the 19th July he was taken up by Lt. Corigan, who demonstrated V formation to echelon and changing leader. His next flight that day was to practice solo, and then later that day to fly solo while being checked by Lt. Ganchow.

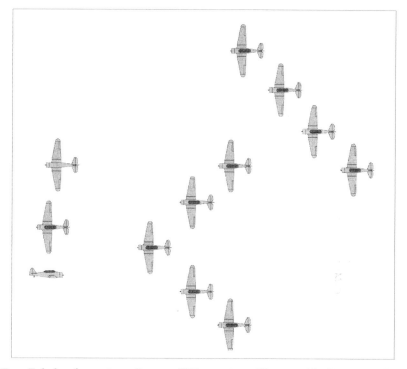

Top: Echelon formation   Bottom: V Formation.   Illustrated by Dave Hatchard

There were regular checks on his progress by other instructors during this period, and at the end of his training at USNAS Grosse Ile, Wright had completed 91 flying hours and was given an assessment: Flying Ability Grade 1.

This was the end of his training with Lt. Tebo, who before writing in his log book remarked that he knew Wright's father was a clergyman and asked how many Psalms there were in the Bible. Wright told him there were 150 Psalms and Lt. Tebo said, 'Well, here is the 151st Psalm?' and wrote:

'Remember the 151st Psalm:
Keep thine Air Speed, lest the ground rise up and smite thee,
BUT HARD!!!
Rules for Living: 1. Control your emotions
2. Think independently
3. Act Courageously
A Pilot is as good as his ability to make a smooth turn.'

Signed: *Vernon Tebo   29 July 1943.*

Lt. Tebo shook hands with Geoff Wright and wished him good luck for the next part of his training.

Off Duty

There were periods of free time when students were able to meet and make friends with local people. While as an Officer Cadet, Geoffrey Wright met some American friends when he visited the Caribou Inn, Clarkston, Michigan, which was approximately 66 miles from Grosse Ile.

The Caribou Inn, Clarkston, Michigan (1925).   Courtesy of Paul Petosky.

The Caribou Inn with Officer Cadet Wright and family group (1943).
Notice the white band on his hat denoting Officer Cadet.
Geoffrey Wright Collection

Quite a number of the American instructors had already been in combat and were sent to the training centres, sometimes finding they were stuck there for a long period, but many, including Lt. Tebo would request to be allowed to return to combat service.

End of training at USNAS Grosse Ile

After his time at USNAS Grosse Ile, Wright transferred to Saufley Field, Pensacola, FLA for Intermediate Training with 2B NAS Saufley:

> 'This was another train journey which took us three days and we had to sleep in our seats. We could not stretch our legs because the train did stop at stations. When we arrived at Saufley Field we were welcomed and shown our accommodation, which was excellent, and in Florida it was a very nice climate to work in and averaged at 32°C in August.'

CHAPTER 5

Intermediate Training, Saufley Field and Whiting Fields, Florida, from August 1943

Saufley Field opened in 1940 with instrument training undertaken at Chevalier Field. The basic training squadron 2B with its Vultee SNV trainers moved to Saufley Field in November 1942. In 1943 the station was commissioned as the Naval Auxiliary Air Station, Saufley Field, for the initial primary training of student naval aviators with Squadron 3-B, beginning operations on 1st July 1943. Just six months later 3B Squadron joined with Squadron 3A, who had been based at Chevalier Field, to move to the newly opened NAAS Whiting Field. Chevalier Field was established in 1922 and had been the original non-seaplane aircraft airfield at Naval Air Station Pensacola, Florida.

The Vultee BT-13A Valiant was a basic trainer aircraft built by Vultee Aircraft originally for the US Army Air Corps, and later US Army Air Forces. The US Navy became interested and ordered BT 13A models, which were then designated SNV-1. The aircraft acquired the nickname 'Vibrator' mainly because it would shake violently, warning the pilot that they were approaching stall speed.

The BT 13A was a two-seat monoplane trainer with the enclosed cockpit doing away with the open cockpits. The aircraft was 29ft 10ins (8.79m) in length, and 12ft 6ins (3.51m) in height, with a wingspan of 42ft (12.8m). It was powered by a Pratt-Whitney R-985-AN-1 Wasp Junior radial, giving a maximum speed of 180 mph (290 kph), a range of 725 miles (1167km) and a ceiling of 21,650ft (6600m).

The Vultee SNV-2 model BT-13B was only different from the BT-13A because it had a 24-volt electric system.

Vultee SNV-2: The photograph of the SNV-2 shows a cadet under instruction with his flying instructor, Keith Lawler, sitting in the rear cockpit.   Joe Lawler Collection

Capt. Keith F. Lawler
Collection of Capt. Keith F. Lawler Sr. USMC/Naval Air, Madison, Wisconsin

Keith Lawler joined the US Marine Corps shortly after the Japanese attack on the US Fleet at Pearl Harbour. He became one of the Flight Instructors at Pensacola Naval Air Station, retiring after the war as Captain Keith Lawler.

One of his sons, Joe Lawler, comments on the father he remembers, 'Five of us sons also served in the military. Oddly, none of his children learned to fly.' Captain Keith Lawler passed away in August 2009, at the age of 88.

Intermediate Training

At first, the intermediate training was reviewing the skills learned in Primary Training, then the student would be introduced to their next aircraft, which was much heavier than the Primary Trainers and also much more powerful. Initial ground instruction was given to the pilots and included an introduction to instrument training. This was to be initiated in the link trainer, practicing 'under-the-hood' flying. The training was first to give the student initial familiarization with instruments and their use in all the various flying manoeuvres. The instrument flying programme began with basic familiarization with instruments and their part in trimming, straight, smooth flight, climbs, glides, spirals, stalls and spins, intricate patterns and recovery from unusual situations procedures. As well as instrument flying, there was the introduction to radio ranging, beam navigation, 'bracketing the beam' and methods of orientation. The final checks include demonstration of primary skills, navigation, instrument flying and landing with instruments.

'On arrival at Saufley Field we had to go through the usual ground instruction before going up in the training aircraft. I was first taken up by Ensign Manheim for familiarization, practice formation work, night flying solo and as a passenger for a formation flight.

On the 9th August 1943, I was given familiarization for flying the SNV No 12931 by Ensign Manheim as the pilot, with me sitting in the trainee cockpit. I was given instruction in flaps and propeller pitch, which was not part of the training we received on the earlier aircraft that were made of wood and canvas, and from now on the aircraft would be of all metal construction. The flying instruction I received was given by four officers, Ensigns Manheim, Codding, Scott and Olmstead.'

Frank Stovin-Bradford, who was a close friend of Geoffrey Wright, remembers when he went to get in the SNV at Saufley Field that there was a large notice with the warning 'DO NOT SPIN!' When he asked what it meant he was told, 'Because it doesn't recover'!

On August 16th Wright was taken up by Ensign Olmstead for night flying practice and practising landings, and this was intermixed with review practice on formation flying and night flying.

Wright commented on the confidence he had gained in flying since starting his training at USNAS Grosse Ile with Lt. Tebo:

'I felt very confident in my flying, which seem to come quite naturally to me, and had no problems during my training with Lt. Tebo. I could confidently take off and land, and practiced touch and go frequently, including taxiing from the apron to take off.

There were frequent checks made by the instructors to confirm whether or not a pilot was fit to go solo or would need to continue with more instruction. I was cleared for fitness to fly and had my final check before starting my formation flying:

This was a three plane V formation flying, which could be very dangerous if any of their wings touched, but was leading to step up/step down to echelon flying and flying side by side until break away.'

The military V formation is similar to watching birds flying in a V formation. The aim was to maintain visual contact and also save fuel, but it was not easy for the two planes flying behind the lead plane. The concentration of the two wingmen found them constantly having to ensure they did not fly into the lead plane, leaving only the lead plane to watch out for the enemy fighters.

V-Formation. Capt. Keith F. Lawler Sr. USMC/Naval Air Madison, Wisconsin

Echelon is a flight formation in which each aircraft flies either to the right (right echelon) or left (left echelon) and maintains a certain height, either above or below and at a certain distance behind the aircraft ahead. The word 'echelon' comes from the French échelle, meaning ladder, describing the effect when viewed from above or below.

Echelon formation.   Capt. Keith F. Lawler Sr.

View from rear cockpit.　　　　　　*Pilot's view from the cockpit.*
Capt. Keith F. Lawler Sr.　　　　　　　*Keith F. Lawler Sr.*

'It was considered by some trainees that night flying in the USA was much easier than the UK where there were the wartime blackouts at night. In the USA the lights were on in the towns and on the roads, so to some extent night flying appeared much easier, until of course going cross-country where the   distances could be quite extensive.

I found some of the night flying terrified me, but I focused on remembering where the airfield was to get back and land. The step down formation and cross under to echelon was the early preparation for landing on carriers or bombing missions, and after completing these manoeuvres I had my final formation check.

My final flight was as a passenger with a chase pilot in a formation flight where the planes are flying behind each other with the leader in the front, and used for various flying procedures. I completed my training at NAS Saufley, FLA on the 27th August 1943 and the next part of my training was to continue at Whiting Field.'

Whiting Field for Instrument Flying Training 1 Sept. 1943

Naval Air Station Whiting Field, in Milton, Florida, was established as a naval air auxiliary station in July 1943. It was Squadron 3A that had transferred from Chevalier Field to form Training Squadron 3, that Wright joined.

Aircraft Flown SNJ

The North American AT-6 was known to the USAAF as the 'AT-6 Texan', the US Navy as the 'SNJ' and the British as the 'Harvard'. SNJ-1s were first delivered in May 1939 to Naval Air Station (NAS) Pensacola, Florida, and by 1943 SNJs were also found at auxiliary bases, including Naval Auxiliary Air Stations (NAAS) Barin Field and Saufley Field, at both of which Wright did some of his flying training.

The North American Aviation SNJ trainer was the primary pilot instruction trainer. The SNJ was 29ft 6ins (8.9m) in length, and 11ft 9ins (3.58m) in height, and with a 42.25ft (12.8m) wing span. The aircraft had retractable landing gear, metal fuselage and power increased by a 550hp Pratt and Whitney R-1340-AN-1 Wasp radial piston engine, giving a maximum speed of 205 mph (330 km/h), a range of 750 miles (1,207m) and a ceiling of 21,500ft (6,555m). The training aircraft had no armaments.

SNJ over NAAS Corry Field.   *John Voss Collection*

The SNJ was seen by the pilots as having a superb cockpit with the undercarriage lever to pull up the retractable undercarriage, excellent brakes, and the vision out of the aircraft was very good. However, there was not going to be much vision out of the aircraft because the students would be undertaking their 'under the hood' instrument training in the SNJ.

Whiting Field

During the period from 1st September to 21st September, the pilots in training were given ground instruction for training in instrument flying, including under the hood, beam flying and radar classroom instruction, the work they would be undertaking at Whiting Field. For this month it was a balance of Link Trainer and instructors piloting the SNJ and demonstrating flying skills, some of which the trainee would practice in the Link Trainer.

On the 21st September Wright commenced his familiarization in a Link Trainer. The Link Trainer was designed and developed by Edwin Link in 1929 to give a trainee pilot experience in simulated flight conditions and instrument training on the ground. Edwin Link was originally an organ builder and used his knowledge of pneumatic bellows to create a flight simulator that would respond to a trainee pilot's controls, to create pitch and roll. He was also the first to fit instruments to his trainers to teach instrument flying, and his Link Trainers became the principal mechanical pilot trainer in the Second World War.

The morning of the 23rd September, Wright was in the Link Trainer for practicing turns, climbs, glides, climbing turns and spins.

Later that day he was taken up by Ensign Mannheim, who was to pilot the aircraft. Familiarization was given on the SNJ No 05637, based on straight level flight and turns while 'under the hood'. This was when a hood was pulled over so that the pilot could not see out and causing him to fly on instruments.

'Under the Hood' is when the pilot is wearing a hood that restricts his visibility out of the cockpit while practicing instrument flying. The pilot's vision is restricted to the portion of the instrument panel in front of him, and can be with full panel or partial panel view for different manoeuvres that the trainee is tasked to do. Some simulated practice would be done in the Link Trainer and some in flight with the instructor. Wright found this quite frightening:

'We were completely blind and had to rely on instrument flying and I found it at first quite horrible, and it was quite frightening when the instructor threw the plane around and upset the giro as a test for us to get out of the problem.'

The pilot had to keep a close eye on the altimeter to check his height and also his airspeed, which brought back memories to Wright of Lt. Tebo's words: 'Keep thine Air Speed, lest the ground rise up and smite thee, BUT HARD!!!'

SNJ NAAS Whiting Field   *John Voss Collection*

The next day, the pilot of the SNJ No 6775 was Ensign Wood, who demonstrated instrument flying, full panel, unusual attitudes, timed turns, climbs, glides and patterns. Later that day it was back to the Link Trainer, for Wright to practice timed turns, climbs and glides, followed the next day with further practice on turns and patterns.

From the 24th to 25th September it was practice in the link trainer on timed turns, climbing and gliding turn, and patterns. On the morning of the 26th September it was in the Link Trainer for an introduction to beam flying familiarization and bracketing the beam.

Beam flying (bracketing the beam) was practised where a pilot would switch onto the beam and wait until he heard a sound, which at first could be intermittent, but once on full beam the pilot would get a continuous sound in his earphones to guide him while he watched his compass closely to maintain his directional flight.

This training was followed by Ensign Marchese taking him up in SNJ No 51575 for instruction in partial panel instrument flying and patterns. Then it was back on the 27th September, first to the Link Trainer for practice in radar flying, and after that session Wright was taken up by Lt. Elliott for demonstrations in unusual attitudes, climbs, glides, slow and fast level cruise and partial panel flying.

Unusual attitudes occurs when a pilot is feeling uncomfortable and close to loss of control through situations occurring such as being distracted, air disturbance, disorientation in cloud or even mechanical failure, and recovery of the aircraft to straight and level flight is required urgently by the pilot. For the trainee pilot it is necessary for them to learn the skills required to get out of such stressful and dangerous situations. The training for full and partial panel, when the trainee pilot is first 'under the hood' would find them feeling quite stressed and getting them to focus on the instruments was the aim. At first the instructors would demonstrate the possible scenarios for unusual attitudes that could occur with partial and full panel, and then the trainee would start to learn the recovery techniques.

For the next two days Wright returned to the Link Trainer for beam flying, then SNJ No 6984 with Ensign Rooney for speed and height changes, climbing and gliding patterns. To complete the months training, on the 29th September it was back to the Link Trainer for close-in procedure in beam flying and later taking to the air in SNJ No 51594 with Lt. Davies for instruction in recovering from unusual positions by partial panel and patterns.

The summary for September recorded that he had flown both the SNJ-3 and SNJ-4. The grand total of flying hours by the end of the month was 132hrs 30mins.

From the 1st October, Wright continued his work on the Link Trainer for radio let down procedure to airport, and later that day Ensign Montgomery took him up in the SNJ 6775 for climbs, glides, speed changes, steep turns and recovery. For the following days, until the 5th October, there were daily Link Trainer followed by Instructor flights for instrument flying, commencing on the 2nd October with Ensign Wood SNJ No 6984, 3rd October with Ensign Perey SNJ No's 51653 and 51550, 4th October with Ensign Zubon SNJ No 51562 and Ensign Marchese SNJ No 6845, 5th October with Ensign Hutchinson No 6845 and Ensign Ellis SNJ 51594 for final radio check.

The training with Squadron 3A at Whiting Field was completed on the 6th October 1943 with a Grand Total of flying time of 141hrs 30mins.

CHAPTER 6

Squadron 3A Barin Field, Alabama, 6 October 1943

Squadron VN-4D8

Barin Field was developed near Foley Municipal Airport, Alabama, because it was in close proximity with Pensacola. It was opened on the 5th December 1942 and named as the NAAS (Naval Auxiliary Air Station) Barin.

Advanced Flying Training begins at Barin Field

With the opening of Barin in December 1942, Squadron VN-4D8 moved from Bronson Field in 1943 to start to instruct flying trainees who were to become torpedo, bomber and fighter pilots.

The training aircraft at Barin Field during World War II included the SNJ, and some SNVs and N2S Stearmans, but the main trainer was the SNJ. It was a very busy training field and this resulted in many crashes and fatalities leading to one newspaper columnist to refer to the base as 'Bloody Barin'.

SNJ NAAS Barin Field.   *John Voss Collection*

The aim of Barin Field was to ensure that trainees who would be eventually going into battle had the necessary practice and experience in aerobatics to be able to avoid enemy attacks, but also to be able to position themselves so that they could attack the enemy.

Aerobatic Manoeuvres

When Wright arrived at Barin Field it was straight into full ground instruction for the next stage, including returning to the classroom for lectures and theoretical studies for his forthcoming flight training.

The first flight for Wright was on the 23rd October with Ensign Ochsenreiter in an SNJ-4 No 27416 for stalls and spins (2x left, 2x right) while he was in the rear cockpit:

'Then it was my first experience of sitting in the front cockpit for take-off and landings. Later that day I went solo to practice take offs and landings while the instructor observed me from the ground.'

On October 25th Wright returned for a session in the N2S-1 No 51923, where the instructor, Ensign Smoot, checked him out on an inverted spin, which he had to undertake two times. Checks by instructors were made on all aerobatics from the ground. All of this flying was undertaken solo and continued on throughout October.

Ensign McReynolds took Wright up in the SNJ No 26854 for loops, slow roll, wingovers, Immelmann turns and 2-turn precision spins completed four times. On the 27th October Wright went up for a solo check and precision landings, while the instructor observed from the ground. From the 27th to 28th October Wright practised all the aerobatic manoeuvres he had experienced with the instructors, and on the 29th October he had an aerobatic check from an instructor on the ground, including, loop, slow roll and Immelmann turn.

Formation Flying

From the 30th October through to 2nd November the focus of the work was on formation flying, starting with 3-plane step-down formation with the instructor leading, steep and shallow turns, breakaway from V to echelon and column and then join up. While practising these manoeuvres the instructor was in a chase aircraft.

'In one session I had to land with a broken oil pipe and could not continue with the flight. Our training continued with a 3-plane formation check by the instructor.'

The summary for October with Squadron VN-4D8 concluded with flights in N2S-1 and SNJ and a total of 163hr 45mins.

From the 3rd to 4th November Wright was flying solo for 6 plane two section formation flying with fighter opposition, including fighter formation for fuel economy with the instructors leading.

Instrument and Night Flying

The next stage was instrument take-offs with Ensign Rhodes in SNJ No 51837 demonstrating instrument take off, turns, climbs and glides on partial panel on the 8th November, and similar flights took place a few days later, flown with instructors Ensign Walker in SNJ No 51889 and Ensign Nott in SNJ No 51959, followed by Wright taking off for solo night flying. Instructors Captain Chamberlain in SNJ No 51496, Ensign Morgan in SNJ No 51766 continued with the instrument flying instruction, and further practice on solo night landings and take-offs were practiced.

Use of Armaments

The first medium altitude strafing runs were led by the instructor, and then in the first strafing practice runs 80 rounds were used. This was followed by Lt. Massie in SNJ No 27325 demonstrating various attack manoeuvres followed by Wright practicing these manoeuvres. By the 20th November the number of hits on targets was recorded. For example, after firing 78 rounds 11 hits were recorded and the next recording of 80 rounds with 10 hits.

For some of the firing practice Wright was tasked to tow a target for the other trainees to fire at. However, for some of the firing sessions problems occurred with poor weather, bad visibility and also guns jamming. By the end of November the flying hours recorded were 210hrs 45mins.

The firing practice continued into December and then it was primary combat against instructors, followed by trainees against trainees, and then a final check on primary combat. These practice combat sessions were thought to be 'very exciting' by Wright and his colleagues.

Bombing Practice

The bombing practice started as usual by a demonstration by Ensign Ochsenreiter in SNJ No 51486, who gave a glide bombing demonstration, followed by Wright practising nine dummy glide bombing runs, all downwards, progressing to dropping five practice bombs. Following on from glide bombing downward runs, it was practice of cross wind and up wind runs. By this time it was flying every day, some in the morning and some in the afternoon, with ground school arranged between flying times.

Navigation

From the middle of December it was practice with their crew on geographic sector searches, first overland and then over water, and finding their way back to the airfield by beam. On the 24th December the over water relative sector search was called off because of bad weather.

This was the final training Wright was to receive at Barin Field, and a check on power and gliding landings, slow rolls, spins and steep turns was undertaken by Lt. Commander MacWhirter with the log book signed off on the 31st December 1944. Lt. Commander MacWhirter was the Senior British Naval Officer, Pensacola, Florida.

Summary for December: Aircraft flown were N2S, SNV and SNJ. Total flying hours of 240hrs 15mins were recorded in the log book.

On the 1st January 1944 Wright was passenger in a C47 flown by Lt. Haverill for a local flight for testing compass, and Lt.

Commander MacWhirter signed Geoff Wright's log book on the 4th January 1944, for the confirmation of his qualification for the Award of Flying Badge.

Lt. Commander R. MacWhirter, Senior British Naval Officer, Pensacola, Florida

Lt. Commander Robert MacWhirter was an expert Supermarine Walrus amphibian biplane pilot and saw service in Norway and the North Atlantic before becoming an instructor at the Empire Central Flying School, and then to Pensacola, Florida, where from July 1943 to September 1944 he was Senior British Naval Officer.

Lt. Commander MacWhirter later returned to operational flying in a Mark IX Spitfire, and in March 1945 took command of 1771 Naval Air Squadron, flying Fireflies from the fleet carrier HMS *Implacable*, and sailed to join the British Pacific Fleet as part of the Sixth Carrier Air Group. He took part in attacks on the Japanese base at Truk in June 1945.

CHAPTER 7

Naval Air Station Fort Lauderdale, Florida, 6 January, 1944

After Wright had left Pensacola, Florida, in January 1944, with 240hrs 15mins of flight training flying, he went to Fort Lauderdale for operational training on Avengers.

Naval Air Station Fort Lauderdale was an airfield of the United States Navy just outside Fort Lauderdale, Florida. In 1942 the navy selected Merle Fogg Airport in Fort Lauderdale to expand into a naval air station for pilots and aircrew training that included radiomen and gunners in Grumman TBF Avenger torpedo bombers, flown by carrier-based US Navy flight crews and by land-based US Marine Corps flight crews ashore. Additional facilities were used to train aircraft maintenance and other ground crew support for the Grumman TBF-1 (1941) and General Motors Co TBM-1 (1942) series aircraft.

Among the Avenger pilots who graduated NAS Fort Lauderdale was George H. W. Bush, who was later to become the 41st President of the United States. George H. W. Bush joined the US Navy in 1942 and was to become the youngest naval aviator in June 1943. While flying Avengers with VT-51 from USS *Jacinto* he was shot down over Chichi Jima, but managed to parachute safely from the aircraft and was rescued. Sadly none of his crew survived.

Grumman TBF Avenger-torpedo bomber

The Grumman TBF Avenger was a torpedo bomber developed initially for the United States Navy and Marine Corps. It was to replace the Douglas TBD-1 Devastator as a torpedo bomber and entered service in 1942 just in time for six TBF-1 Avengers to take part in the Battle of Midway on 4th June 1942. The TBF-1 Avengers were bigger, faster and had a longer range that the TBD Devastator Torpedo Squadron VT-8. The squadron had already sailed on the aircraft carrier USS *Hornet* for Midway when the

TBF-1 Avengers arrived at Pearl Harbour. Six of the TBFs took off under the command of Lt. Langdon K. Fieberling, with none of the pilots having experienced combat and arrived over the Japanese fleet early in the morning, attacking at a low altitude. Without fighter cover they were attacked by Japanese Zeros and five of the six aircraft were shot down. The VT-8 Squadron flying TBD Devastator also joined the battle for their first combat mission from the USS *Hornet*, but all fifteen aircraft were shot down.

The Royal Navy's Fleet Air Arm was in need of a more modern and effective torpedo bomber and received from the USA the first batch of just over 400 TBF 1s, which they designated 'Tarpon I' and modified for use by the British pilots.

Although some Avengers served on a number of escort carriers in the British Home Fleet and with Coastal Command in the D-Day landings, its main contribution was in the Far East, and proved to be a very effective in its role with the Fleet Air Arm and the British Pacific Fleet. The designation 'TBM' was for Avengers manufactured by General Motors when production started in 1943. This was due to Grumman concentrating on the production of F6F Hellcat fighters.

TBF Avenger Torpedo Bomber

Grumman TBF-1 torpedo bomber with three crew, consisting of
pilot, radio operator and gunner.   Geoffrey Wright

TBF-1 was a torpedo bomber that was 40ft 11ins (12.47m) in length and 16ft 5ins (5m), with a wing span of 54ft 2ins (16.51m) powered by a 1,900hp Wright R-2600-20 Twin Cyclone radial engine at a cruise speed of 147mph (236 km/h) to a maximum speed of 276 mph (444 kp/h), with a range with internal tanks of 1,010 miles (1626 km) and a ceiling of 30,100ft (9174m), and had folding wings. It carried a crew of three, with pilot, bomb-aimer and radio operator, and gunner. Its armaments consisted of a 0.30 nose mounted machine gun used by the pilot, one 0.30 machine gun in the powered rear turret for rear gunner, and one 0.30 machine gun in the lower belly. These weapons were updated as the newer variants of the Avenger appeared. There was a large weapons bay that could carry a torpedo or four 500lb (225kg) bombs. One major advantage was that the Avenger was a very rugged aircraft that could sustain intensive battle damage, protecting aircrew while being still able to fly.

The Grumman Avenger was the most important attack aircraft for the East Indies Fleet and the British Pacific Fleet when the Royal Navy returned to the Far East in 1944 and 1945. At first the TBF-1 Avengers were given the designation 'Tarpon I-III' and this continued until January 1944 when the Fleet Air Arm reverted again to the American name 'Avenger'.

Training starts at Fort Lauderdale

Result of a day's fishing on the boat 'Dorothy'.
GW Collection

Geoffrey Wright, standing far left.
GW Collection

Geoffrey Wright started at NAS Fort Lauderdale on the 6th January 1944, and until the 14th January took part in ground instruction and classroom work introducing the TBF Avenger that they were to fly. There was some interesting leisure time while there, including fishing and driving around in an American car.

Period for January 14 – March 5, 1944.
Flying mainly TBF, but also SNJ

The first flight was for familiarization and flown solo for climbs, glides, stalls and steep turns. Some of the flights were solo, but on the 23rd January Lt. Reichers took Wright up in the SNJ No 26506 for instrument flying, take off demonstration, climbs, glides, power changes, emergency landing procedures, S-turns and spirals. Gradually the crew were part of the flights and so the teamwork started to develop. Work during January focused on; anti-submarine glide bombing, dropping 8x100lb bombs, high altitude flying with oxygen, radio practice and strafing runs for the tunnel and turret gunners. Further formation flying was practiced, homing in on ships at sea, night flying, anti-submarine glide bombing, dropping 6 bombs and scoring 6 hits, including low level anti-sub bombing on a moving target, torpedo practice and evasive action against fighter attack. For one flight, oil on the windshield forced Wright an early return.

Wright talks about some of the flying skills he was practicing for his future combat role:

'We did further practice on instrument flying, but this was within cumulus clouds and high altitude flying at 18,000 feet with oxygen, putting our masks on at 12,000ft and switching on the oxygen. It was important to get your Green Ticket. All FAA pilots had to be tested in flying in cloud. The maximum height for the Avenger was 21,750ft.

Low flying over water at 50ft-100ft was very difficult, especially when flying at night. It must also be remembered that aerobatics practice for combat depends on what you are flying. A fighter, because of its speed, needs to be able to get out of trouble quickly, but something like an Avenger is a heavier plane and usually to get out of trouble the pilot would pull up and go into a loop, or dive steeply towards the ground or sea and then at the last moment pull back. Fighter attack evasive action is to either go straight up or dive down to the sea, but the pilot of the fighter would have to be aware that in a dive the fighter is much faster than the Avenger, and he may not be able to pull back in time and crash into the ground or sea.'

At the end of the month the summary included flights in SNJ and TBF and a total of 260hrs 25mins and was signed by Lt. Cdr. Kindell, Chief Instructor, RN VTB Training USA.

From the 1st to 4th February 1944 Wright was joined by his crew for anti-sub bombing on moving target, dummy torpedo attack, free and fixed gunnery against towed target and high level glide bombing from 6,000ft to 2500ft dropping 6 bombs on still target, gunnery practice for low level strafing and runs on towed targets.

On the 5th February, Ensign Burgins took Wright up in SNB No 39207 for radar familiarization, homing in on ships at sea. The Beechcraft SNB was a twin engine bomber that was mainly used for flying above and observing trainee TBF pilots and identifying bombing and torpedo strikes. Continuing on from February 6th, more bombing practice, including homing flights undertaken three times and night flying with touch and go landings.

Then it was back to the Link Trainer for radio beam orientation and practice navigation flight-relative sector search, and then for the next five days it was flying solo in the TBF for dummy torpedo runs on ship, night flying familiarization and touch and go landings. This was until the 17th February when the aircrew joined him for fixed and free gunnery run, and it was noted that 'all guns fired', and they also practised high altitude glide bombing on moving target with six bombs.

Later in the month there were instructor flights in the SNJ. The first was with Capt. French in SNJ No 05518, Lt. Moore in SNJ No 01905, and Ensign Sellers in SNJ No 26506, who demonstrated instrument flight, simulated emergency landing and fighter evasion tactics. On the 25th February, Lt. Merrill in SNJ No 05518 undertook a check on Wright's progress.

Then it was back to more bombing practice, which Wright remembers well:

'Further bombing practice took place, but after using dummy concrete torpedoes, we used a live torpedo with dummy warhead, but I missed the target which was 50ft ahead.

The rest of February included ADDLs (Aerodrome Dummy Deck Landings) which were practising deck landings on land before attempting on an aircraft carrier. There was the ADDL landing control officer on the runway and we landed hook down on the runway with a three-point landing. The USS landing officer did the reverse of a Fleet Air Arm landing officer, and so we were taught the American way.

When we went to Lewiston, we were taught the British way of deck landing.'

The summary for the end of February at USNAS Fort Lauderdale confirmed flights in TBF and SNJ with a total of 336hr 10mins and was signed by Lt. Cdr. Kindell Chief Instructor RN VTB Training USA.

Wright explains how the pilot and aircrew worked together for the practice flights:

'I would do regular practice runs on anti-submarine glide bombing with the crew, including the navigator/radioman, and gunners, to practice strafing runs for the tunnel and turret gunners. This led to practice anti-sub attacks with bombs against a moving target, and the very important practice of evasive action from fighter attacks.

Other practice included further bombing and strafing attacks from different altitudes, including dummy torpedo attacks on moving targets. Glide bombing depended on the type of target, whether it was a moving tank, static AA guns, or ships and submarines at sea.

When firing at towed targets, all Avengers were provided with five different coloured bullets which after the exercise could be checked to assess the number of hits the pilot gets on the target.

I would first have an instructor flight for radar familiarization and homing in on ships at sea, and solo night flying, touch and go landings, and radio beam orientation. Following on from the instructor flights and solo flying practice, I would take the aircrew up for gunnery practice and bombing. One important night flying learning skill we were shown and practised, was finding the direction of the wind, and one way of finding that was by looking at the direction of the smoke from the ships' funnels.

In preparation for landing on aircraft carriers, we would undertake many ADDLs (Aerodrome Dummy Deck Landings) to give us plenty of practice before our first attempts at landing on an aircraft carrier.'

The Fleet Air Arm pilots were training at the same time as the US Navy trainees and photograph records were taken of these groups.

British Fleet Air Arm Trainees and US Navy Trainees with their US instructors.
Geoffrey Wright is third from left in back row.
Geoffrey Wright Collection

Fleet Air Arm Trainees with their US Instructors.
Geoffrey Wright is third from left in back row.
Geoffrey Wright Collection

The final entries in the log book recorded 15 ADDLs for March 4th and 18 ADDLs for March 5th.

This was the end of the training at USNAS Fort Lauderdale, and on the 5th March 1944 Wright completed his RN VTB (Torpedo-Bombing) Course and his ability as VTB Pilot was assessed as 'Above Average'. He got his wings and became a flying officer. His log confirming the award was signed by Lt. Commander Kindell R.N. Chief Instructor RN VTB Training USN.

From NAS Fort Lauderdale, Sub Lt. (A) Wright RNVR, with a total of 336 flying hours, travelled by rail to Boston, Massachusetts, and then on to USNAS Lewiston, Maine, USA, to continue training on Avenger Torpedo Bombers.

CHAPTER 8

USNAF Lewiston, 738 Squadron
and USNAS Squantum, 857 Squadron

Naval Air Station Brunswick, Maine, was constructed in March 1943 and commissioned on April 15th 1943, to train RN Fleet Air Arm pilots to fly squadrons of the TBF Avengers, F4U Corsair, and F6F Hellcat in the Second World War. USNAF Lewiston was one of five auxiliary fields used to support NAS Brunswick in the training of TBF Avenger torpedo bomber pilots.

Sub. Lt. (A) Wright RNVR, kneeling first left bottom row, with his colleagues after qualification.   *Geoffrey Wright Collection*

After arrival at USNAF Lewiston on the 9th March, Sub. Lt. Wright was back into the classroom until the 14th March for an introduction to the training they were to receive when the practical flying was to start.

At USNAF Lewiston, Maine, Sub. Lt. Wright was familiarized with the local area, flying Avengers with British roundels, learning the British type of formation flying and deck landing, flying formation in cloud, and tail chasing. Further practice was undertaken on low level anti-submarine bombing and low altitude flying over water, steep turns, evasive action and cloud flying. Then there was practice dog-fighting with one other Avenger, and Wright refers to the different types of attacks they had to prepare for:

> 'We practised for high side attack from overhead, flat side attack from same altitude, either straight from behind, or coming in from either side.'

Sub. Lt .(A) Wright RNVR flying TBM Avenger from 738 Squadron, Lewiston, Maine. *Geofrey Wright Collection*

On April 3rd, Sub. Lt. Wright took his aircrew up for night flying

71

familiarization, that included three landings, further work on ADDLS before anti-sub bombing with 8 bombs and dropping two bombs at a time from 50ft. While most of the practices were undertaken from the NAS airfields, Wight remembers the strange field/small field practice:

'That was where we would practice landing on a field where we hadn't been before. That was quite important because it could be emergency where you have engine problem or you could be short of fuel. We would also undertake forced landing practice when damaged through attack, engine problems or out of fuel.'

After much ADDLs (Aerodrome Dummy Deck Landings) it was time to practice the first deck landing on an aircraft carrier.

Final deck landing practice took place on the USS *Charger* in Chesapeake Bay off Norfolk, Virginia, and on the 8 April 1944, Wight made his first four successful landings on USS *Charger*, flying solo TBF JZ337.

The next day was flying in formation from Norfolk back to Lewiston, with Sub. Lt. Baker. Then it was back to solo flying until the middle of April, when it was flying continuously with the aircrew practising Navex (navigation exercise) over land, night flying, low flying and bombing still and moving targets, formation flare dropping at night, finishing up with a 20-plane exercise consisting of 12 TBFs in formation with 8 F4U Corsairs escorting. Sub. Lt. Wright was flying TBF FN 770 with aircrew.

The final flight Sub. Lt. Wright made was in TBF JZ387 when he carried three passengers to USNAS Squantum to collect spare parts and return.

Aircraft flown were listed in Sub. Lt. Wright's log book as 'NPI, N2S, SNV, SNJ and Avenger', with the assessment for Day and Night Flying as a 'Good Average'.

This was the end of the Sub. Lt. Wright's training at USNAF Lewiston with 738 Squadron. His logbook was signed off by Squadron Commander Tattersall Lt. (A) RN. D.S.C. on the 29th April 1944. Total Flying Hours 375hrs.

857 Squadron USNAS Squantum, Boston, 13 May, 1944

It was at USNAS Squantum that the Fleet Air Arm squadrons 851 through to 857 were formed at monthly intervals from the start of 851 Naval Air Squadron on the 1st October 1943. Each of the squadrons would then sail to the UK with their aircraft on an escort carrier, with the exception of 854 Squadron, which sailed on HMS *Indomitable*.

851 Squadron sailed on the escort carrier HMS *Shah*, 852 Squadron on HMS *Nabob*, 853 Squadron on HMS *Arbiter*, 854 Squadron on HMS *Indomitable*, 855 Squadron on HMS *Queen*, 856 Squadron on HMS *Smiter*, and finally 857 Squadron on HMS *Rajah*.

857 Naval Air Squadron was the last squadron to be formed on the 1st April 1944 at USNAS Squantum, Boston, as an Avenger torpedo bomber reconnaissance squadron. The Commanding Officer was Lt. Cdr. (A) W 'Doc' Stuart RNVR.

This was the time when Sub. Lt. (A) Frank Stovin-Bradford remembers meeting up with his old colleagues who had been training in the USA and were now all members of 857 Squadron. They included, Geoffrey Wright, Harry Smith, Derrick Langshaw, Peter Thompson, Tom Staniforth, Danny Buchanan and Robin Hibburd, who sadly was lost in the raid on Palembang, Sumatra, on the 24th January 1945. Sub. Lt. (A). Frank Stovin-Bradford became the Division Officer for the squadron, which was mainly an administrative job. The squadron consisted of 12 Avengers, 12 pilots, observers and gunners, and 102 ground crew including (mechanics, fitters, electricians etc).

After joining 857 Naval Air Squadron at USNAS Squantum it was ten days of class based work and then back to practical work. Sub. Lt. Wright spent his first session in the Link Trainer where he did two exercises on radio procedure. The first flight on May 24th was with his crew and Sub. Lt. Glendinning, navigator, and L/A Esson, gunner, in TBF No JZ401for familiarization of area around Boston.

The rest of the month was with his aircrew undertaking Navex (Navigation exercise) either over land or over sea. This Navex was to be over sea in formation and at low altitude, practising radio procedure, and a bombing practice with 6 bombs over the Cape Cod area with Sub. Lt. Beeny and L/A Esson as crew.

Sub. Lt. (A) Frank Stovin-Bradford RNVR piloting TBM JZ497 from USNAS Squantum for ADDL practice on May 12th 1944. GW Collection

From the 1st June Sub. Lt. Wright and his crew changed over to flying the TBM, built by General Motors, and continued with full aircrew on bombing runs in the Cape Cod area and gunnery practice using two .5 wing guns, turret and tunnel guns. Then it was night Navex over sea with return to fictitious ship, but they encountered storm and lightning conditions and had to climb above it. On the 14th June, Sub. Lt. Wright was just taking off when an ammunition cover broke loose and they had to return to the airfield. Later that day it was formation flare dropping, followed by a solo flare dropping exercise. The final flight of US training was a low level (100ft) formation Navex, but the logbook stated 'bad weather caused speedy return', and listed 406 hours at the end of the US Training.

CHAPTER 9

Return to the United Kingdom, July 1944

Showing the Flag

With his training completed in the USA, Sub. Lt. Wright was to return with 857 Squadron and their Avengers to the UK on the Escort Carrier HMS *Rajah*. However, just before 857 Squadron left USNAS Squantum to return to the UK, they had a party. The next morning the Commanding Officer Lt. Cdr. (A) W Stuart RNVR wanted the squadron to see New York and arranged for the whole squadron of 12 Avengers to fly over Manhattan:

'We took off for New York and flew below the level of the Empire State Building, whose 102 floors reached 1,250ft (381m), showing the flag and then flew back to Norfolk, Virginia, and landed. The wings were then folded and all 12 Avengers taxied along the streets to the docks, causing quite an interest with the people of Norfolk, especially with the gusts of wind that were coming from the 12 propellers.

We embarked on HMS *Rajah* at the Naval Base, Norfolk, Virginia on the 29th June 1944 and at the same time our 12 Avengers were loaded on board. As well as our squadron, 1842 Squadron with their 18 Corsairs were on board to travel back to the UK with us.'

Once all the embarkation had been completed and all aircraft and stores loaded, HMS *Rajah* set sail for New York where she joined the Convoy TCU-30 on the 2nd July. USS *Howard D. Crow* DE-252 was one of the 12 American escort vessels that sailed with Convoy TCU-30, leaving New York on the 2nd July 1944 for the UK, and was attached to the convoy until they reached the coast of Ireland on the 11th July 1944 without incident.

The convoy of 38 ships was made up of a variety of merchant ships and included 12 passenger/troopships. On arrival at Liverpool on the 12th July, 1842 Squadron and their Corsairs were

75

unloaded. HMS *Rajah* then set sail for Belfast, arriving on the 13th July, where 857 Squadron disembarked and their Avengers were unloaded. The next voyage for HMS *Rajah* would be when she set sail from Belfast on the 10th September bound for India and Ceylon, and one of the squadrons on board would be 857 Squadron. From the period July to September 1944 HMS *Rajah* would spend some time as a Deck Landing Training Carrier.

857 Squadron RNAS Belfast N.I. 27 July 1944-5 August 1944

Belfast Airport became operational as 'RAF Belfast' in 1941 and was transferred to the Admiralty and commissioned in late 1943 as 'HMS Gadwell'. It was used by the Fleet Air Arm for disembarking squadrons and aircraft maintenance.

On the 30th July 1944, Sub. Lt. Wright and his aircrew flew in TBM JZ401 on a one hour familiarization of the Belfast area of Northern Ireland. On the 7th August 1944 until the 7th September 1944, Sub. Lt. Wright was based with 853 Squadron at RNAS Machrihanish (HMS Landrail) for bombing training with their Avenger torpedo bombers.

Brief history of 853 Squadron based at RNAS Machrihanish (HMS Landrail)

The Commanding Officer of 853 Squadron, while 857 Squadron was based at RAF Machrihanish in 1944, was Lt. Cdr. R.N. Haig RNVR.

853 Squadron was formed at USNAS Squanton in December 1943 as an Avenger torpedo bomber reconnaissance squadron, with Lt. Cdr. N. G. Haig as Commanding Officer. In April 1944 they flew from USNAS Squanton to the RCAF Sea Island Base, Vancouver, to embark on HMS *Arbiter* for what was to be her maiden voyage. HMS *Arbiter* sailed from Vancouver down the west coast of the USA and through the Panama Canal, continuing up the east coast and calling in at the Norfolk naval dockyard for some repair work before completing its voyage to New York.

While on board during this period, 853 Squadron did plenty of practice in deck landings and generally working up procedures.

However in New York, because HMS *Arbiter* would be taking a deck cargo of Corsairs on board, 853 Squadron Avengers were stored below in a hanger, so no further practice was possible. HMS *Arbiter* left New York on June 6th 1944 (D-Day for the Normandy Landings), joining convoy CU27 and arrived in Glasgow on 20th June, where the Corsairs and Avengers were unloaded. The squadron then flew to RNAS Machrihanish, where they were to be based until joining HMS *Tracker* to take part in escort duties on the Arctic convoys to Russia, and later on HMS *Queen* where the squadron also took part in the last air raid in Europe in the Second World War. This was Operation Judgement, the attack on the Kilbotn U-Boat base, Norway.

Balure Bombing Range

The Balure Range was a World War II live bombing and firing range located on the western coast of the Kintyre peninsula, about three miles west of Campbeltown. The ranges were used for training squadrons posted to HMS Landrail (RNAS Machrihanish), and operated both day and night exercises.

From August 9th through to August 26th, Sub. Lt. Wright and his aircrew were flying in TBM Avenger II JZ572 for bombing practice on the Skipness Bombing Range, dropping four 225 lb depth charges and six practice bombs dropped in pairs on a moving, submerging target while taking evasive action. While on a three plane formation flight the target tow ship did not appear so they had to return to base, but the formation returned later for bombing practice on moving tanks with 3 flash bombs while strafing with a .30 belly gun on the Tarbet-Balure Road. They practiced night flare dropping and 3 plane attacks on submarine and at the end of the training period were dropping live depth charges on towed target. When undertaking live fire and bombing it was the Balure Bombing Range that was used.

After four weeks based at RNAS Machrihanish Sub. Lt. Wright and his aircrew returned to Belfast and his log book was signed off by Lt. Cdr. Haigh RNVR, Commanding Officer of 853 Squadron, with flying hours recorded as 426 hrs 40 mins. That was the end of the training for 857 Squadron in the UK and Sub.

Lt. (A) Geoffrey E. Wright RNVR and his crew returned from RNAS Machrihanish to Belfast:

'When I returned to 857 Squadron it was to embark on the escort carrier HMS *Rajah* that was to transport the squadron to Ceylon. On September 8th, I flew TBM Avenger JZ564 with my aircrew and one passenger from the base to the embarkation point at Belfast.'

On the 9th September, HMS *Rajah* started boarding personnel, aircrew and 12 Avengers of 849 Squadron with Commanding Officer Lt. Cdr. David Foster, aircrew and personnel, 21 Avengers of 857 Squadron with Commanding Officer Lt. Cdr. W Stuart, aircrew and personnel, 888 Squadron, Commanding Officer Lt. Cdr. Mann with their 6 PR (Photographic Reconnaissance) Hellcats, aircrew and personnel. 888 Squadron was the very first Fleet Air Arm PR Squadron and was fitted with vertical cameras in the USA. HMS *Rajah* departed Belfast on the 10th September for Ceylon (Sri Lanka).

Part 2: The War in the Far East and the Pacific

CHAPTER 10

US Embargo on selling oil to Japan

When the Imperial Japanese Military started to seize the Western Colonies in South East Asia, including what was French Indochina (Vietnam), in July 1941, US President Franklin D. Roosevelt imposed an embargo on selling oil to Japan. The British and Dutch also imposed economic sanctions, especially on imports of materials for warfare production, because of the Japanese troops' brutal treatment of the Chinese people.

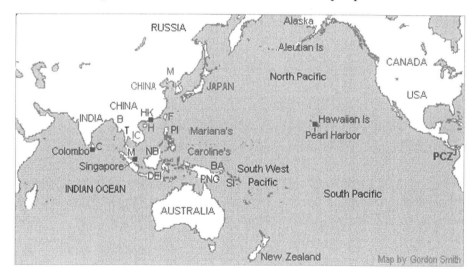

Position of Allies, Axis and neutral countries at beginning of the Far East and Pacific War

Key to map: ***Allies****: B-Burma, BA-Bismarck Arch, C-Ceylon, DEI- Dutch East Indies, HK-Hong Kong, M-Malaya, NB-North Borneo, PI-Philippine Islands, PCZ-Panama Canal Zone, PNG-Papua New Guinea, SI- Solomon Islands.*
Axis: *F-Formosa, H-Hainan, IC-Indo China, K-Korea, M-Manchuria*
Neutral: *T-Thailand*

Courtesy of Gordon Smith   www.naval-history.net

With the economic sanctions on Japan having an effect, it was now plunged into a serious fuel crises because most of its oil was imported and any reserves it had in Japan would not last long without further replenishment. However, the Japanese military hardliners had no intention of giving in to any of the Western Governments, so in July 1941 the Japanese decided to go to war with the United States.

There was no delay in Japan preparing for war, with aircraft undertaking practice attacks on their own fleet in advance of the planned attack on the US Fleet in Pearl Harbour. The Japanese Navy had gained valuable experience from its actions off China, which focused on air strikes that concentrated all the carriers in the fleet working as one and not one carrier acting alone. By the start of the Pacific War in 1941, the Japanese Combined Fleet consisted of 10 aircraft carriers, 10 battleships, 38 heavy and light cruisers and 110 destroyers.

The Imperial Japanese Navy formed the First Air Fleet which combined all the carriers under one command. The new carrier fleet included the *Akagi, Kaga, Hiryu* and *Soryu*, which were the first group that started the practice strikes. They were then joined by the *Shokaku* and *Zuikaku*, and these were the carriers that would be involved in the actual attack on the American Pacific Fleet based at Pearl Harbour.

In October 1941, Hideki Tojo became Prime Minister of Japan and ordered Admiral Isoroku Yamamoto, Commander of the Japanese Combined Fleet, to prepare to launch the attack on Pearl Harbour, the large American naval base in Hawaii. The American Pacific Fleet was thought to be the biggest threat to the Japanese plans for further expansion of its Empire. Admiral Yamamoto was well aware of the increasing strength of the American Pacific Fleet and knew that his plan would have to be so focused and devastating to the Americans that they would find it impossible to recover from the attack.

The attack was planned for December 7th 1941, and the six carriers, the *Akaga, Kaga, Soryu, Hiryu, Shokaku* and *Zuikaku*, along with the seaplane cruisers *Tone* and *Chikuma,* battleships

Hiei and *Kirishima*, one light cruiser and nine destroyers, had been assigned to the operation. In command of naval attack was Admiral Nagumo, with Commander Fuchida, leader of the air mission. Although the attack was devastating to the ships and sailors in Pearl Harbour, it was unable to destroy one of its main targets, which was the aircraft carriers, because they were out at sea on manoeuvres and not in harbour. The attack sank eighteen ships and destroyed approximately 200 aircraft, damaging a further 150, but they did not attack the submarine base, dockyard or fuel supplies.

When Admiral Nimitz arrived at Pearl Harbour shortly after the attack, he could not believe that the Japanese navy had not come back to complete the job. This was something that the Japanese would regret when the United States, thought at the time to be the 'the sleeping giant', was to 'wake up' and declare war on Japan the very next day. Australia, aware of the possible consequences that a war in the Pacific could bring on their country, also declared war on Japan the same day. Just three days later the Germans and the Italians declared war on the United States, and so America was now fully involved in the Second World War.

The British Eastern Fleet

The British Admiralty was aware of the growing danger from Japan early on in the Second World War, and as a result had started to build up the Eastern Fleet, which had been formed with ships from the East Indies Station and China Station with its naval base at Singapore. With the threat by the Japanese fleet of an invasion of Malaya and Singapore, a British fleet, code named 'Z Force' was assembled to be sent to the Far East in 1941.

However, in the build-up of Z Force, its only aircraft carrier, HMS *Indomitable*, hit a reef on the 2nd November 1941, while entering Kingston harbour, Jamaica, and could not take part in Force Z departure. Instead the carrier sailed to Norfolk, Virginia, for repairs to the damage caused by running aground. After repairs HMS *Indomitable* left to join the fleet in Ceylon in December 1941, but was not able to be in position in time to support the defence of Singapore.

The Eastern Fleet, under the command of Admiral Sir Thomas Philips, had set sail on the 8th December 1941 from Singapore in the battleship HMS *Prince of Wales*, with HMS *Repulse* and four destroyers, to attack the Imperial Japanese Navy Forces which had invaded the north-east coast of Malaya. However, the British ships were attacked by a large number of Japanese bombers, but without an aircraft carrier there was no air cover and both the battleship HMS *Prince of Wales* and the battlecruiser HMS *Repulse* were sunk. Admiral Sir Thomas Phillips who was in command of the fleet was lost when he went down with HMS *Prince of Wales*.

The British Eastern Fleet withdrew to Trincomalee, Ceylon, where Admiral Sir James Somerville assumed control.

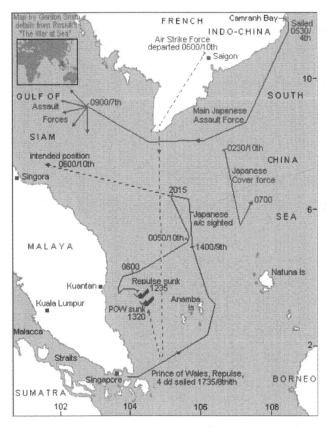

Sinking of HMS Prince of Wales and HMS Repulse
by IJN bombers and torpedo bombers on 10th December 1941.
Courtesy of Gordon Smith - details from Roskill's 'The War at Sea.'

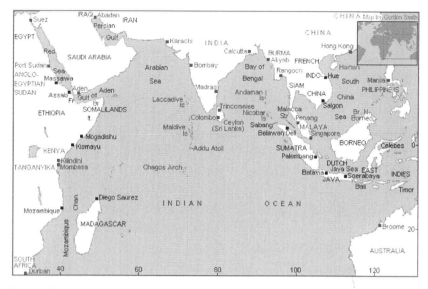

The British Eastern Fleet was based at Trincomalee and took part in action in the Indian Ocean and Bay of Bengal before the formation of the British Pacific Fleet in November, 1944.   *Courtesy of Gordon Smith   www.naval-history.net*

Japan's expanding supply lines

The day after the attack on Pearl Harbour, Japanese bombers and fighters from bases on Formosa carried out air strikes on the US Airfields based in the Philippines, destroying many B-17 bombers and P-40 fighters, virtually half the US Air Force on the islands.

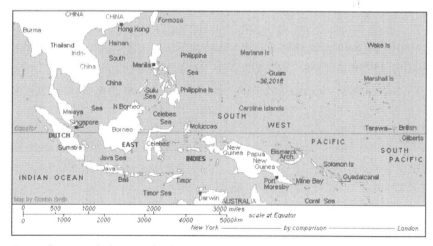

Expanding supply lines and subsequent Japanese attacks on the oil refineries in Sumatra.   *Courtesy of Gordon Smith   www.naval-history.net*

After gaining control of the skies, the Japanese started their invasion of the Philippines, followed by further attacks on Guam and the Wake Islands. The British forces in Hong Kong surrendered to the Japanese on the 26th December 1941, followed by Singapore on the 15th February 1942. The Japanese war machine continued marching on, with amphibious landings in Thailand and Burma, and increasing threats on India and Ceylon. But while extending the Japanese Empire, they also were extending their supply lines, so essential to their homeland and for their forces in the areas they had invaded and captured. After the surrender of British troops in Malaya in 1942, there was only the Dutch East Indies and New Guinea between the advances of the Japanese towards Australia.

With the Japanese Imperial Army and Navy spread even wider as more countries in the Far East were invaded and occupied, there was still the defence of mainland Japan to consider. Capturing the Philippines was important to the Japanese as it was at a strategic location between Japan and the South Pacific, and gaining control through its invasion and occupation opened out a more secure route from the oil fields and refineries of the Dutch East Indies (Indonesia) to Japan.

Invasion of Sumatra

With Japan's need to ensure a regular supply of oil, there was an increasing threat of an invasion of Sumatra, which at the time was part of the Dutch East Indies and had the important Royal Dutch Shell oil refineries at Pladjoe, near Palembang.

A decision was made to build a second airfield in the Palembang area to protect the oil refineries. There was an airfield to the north of Palembang, which was the Pangkalan Benteng airfield, which is the location of the current civilian airport. This was known as the 'P1 Airfield' and the second airfield was the Prabumulih military airfield, known as the 'P2'.

P2 was effectively a secret airfield, because it was well hidden in a jungle clearing, where the aircraft could be hidden under the trees, and it was never discovered by the many Japanese reconnaissance aircraft flights over the area.

The Allies were well aware of the possibility of a Japanese strike, and in January 1942, the decision was made to base RAF and RAAF aircraft in the two airfields P1and P2. On the 18th January 1942, the newly formed 225th RAF Bomber Group, consisting of two RAAF squadrons and RAF squadrons, with a total of 35 Lockheed Hudson and 40 Bristol Blenheim, had moved to Palembang.

The Hurricanes of No.226 RAF (Fighter) Group were based at P1, which had concrete runways and was on the north side of the Musi River. HMS *Indomitable* had transported two squadrons of Hurricanes to Sumatra and these were flown off the carrier on 27 January 1942, for Palembang. However, of the 48 Hurricanes that had arrived, subsequent air combats with Japanese aircraft had left them with just 15 Hurricanes by the time of the invasion.

The KNIL (Royal Netherlands East Indies Army) Territorial Command was based in Palembang to defend the refineries, along with a group of British Royal Artillery soldiers manning the anti-aircraft guns. The Royal Netherlands Navy had the minelayer *Pro Patria* and the patrol boats *P-38* and *P-40* based on the Musi River.

The importance to the Japanese of capturing Palembang was due to the oil embargo placed on Japan by the United States, the Netherlands and Britain, and especially because the Royal Dutch 'Shell' refineries were based at Pladjoe, near Palembang. Gaining control of the oil refineries would be an important addition to the depleted Japanese oil supplies.

The attack on Palembang, southern Sumatra, started on the 13th February 1942, when the Japanese invasion fleet was approaching southern Sumatra. On the 14th February, Allied aircraft took off and attacked the Japanese fleet, sinking one ship and damaging others. While this was ongoing, Japanese transport aircraft delivered the first wave of 180 paratroopers over the P1 airfield while escorted by Nakajima Ki-43 Army fighters (Oscar's) from the 59th and 64th Sentai (Squadrons). A second group of 90 parachutists dropped on the Pladjoe oil refinery, but they were at first driven off by the defenders, who then started to prepare demolition charges to destroy the oil refineries, but these failed, although there were some fires started. In this first attack the Japanese paratroopers were beaten off and had to withdraw to wait for the main attacking force.

Although the paratroopers attacked the airfield, the defence forces had managed to keep the attackers away while RAF aircraft landed, and were able to refuel before taking off again to move to the P2 airfield. Returning Hurricanes were also diverted to P2, refuelled, re-armed, and took off again. Both the defenders at the airfield and at the refinery were also evacuated to P2. The reason that P2 was not attacked by paratroopers was because they did not know of its existence.

The main Japanese invasion force was an amphibious assault against Sumatra, under the command of Vice-Admiral Jisaburo Ozawa, who was in the cruiser *Chokai* and led the 7th Cruiser Squadron. It was positioned at the entrance to Bangka Strait while Japanese forces invaded Bangka Island and for the main force to take Palembang. A brave attack on the invasion fleet was made by the British river boat HMS *Li Wo*, which after being seriously damaged, still rammed a Japanese transport ship before sinking.

Japanese air support was from aircraft off the carrier *Ryujo*, and also the land-based Japanese Army Air Force, while their amphibious forces sailed up the Musi, Salang and Telang rivers to attack Palembang. The Allied aircraft continued to attack the invading amphibious forces, with RAF aircraft bombing the landing craft and sinking the Japanese freighter *Otawa Maru*. The Hurricanes joined in by flying up and down the rivers, machine gunning the Japanese soldiers in the landing craft.

There was an attempt by Admiral Doorman's five cruisers, HNLMS *De Ruyter*, HNMLS *Java*, HMLMS *Tromp*, HMS *Exeter* and HMAS *Hobart*, supported by ten destroyers to intercept Vice Admiral Ozawa's Fleet, but aircraft from the Japanese carrier *Ryujo* and other land-based aircraft attacked the Allied ships and they were forced to withdraw out of the area.

It was all over by the 15th February 1942, when all Allied aircraft were sent to Java, where a Japanese attack was expected, and by the 16th February the Allies had left southern Sumatra for either Java or India. With the other advances made by the Japanese forces to the north, the whole of Sumatra was eventually occupied and in complete control by the Japanese.

HMS *Indomitable* re-joins the British Eastern Fleet

HMS Indomitable　　　　　*Courtesy of Paul Whiteing*

In March 1942 HMS *Indomitable* joined the Eastern Fleet, and after the transportation of Hurricanes to RAF bases, the carrier arrived in Ceylon and commenced operations with Force A of the Eastern Fleet.

Along with the carrier HMS *Formidable*, the battleship HMS *Warspite* and cruisers HMS *Cornwall*, HMS *Dorsetshire*, HMS *Enterprise* and HMS *Emerald*, Force A searched for the Japanese aircraft carriers and warships believed to be preparing for an attack on Ceylon. However, during the search HMS *Formidable* received some damage and had to withdraw and proceed to Bombay for repairs. HMS *Dorsetshire* and her sister ship HMS

Cornwall also left Force A to return to Ceylon, but was spotted by Japanese reconnaissance aircraft, who reported the sighting to the Japanese fleet. Dive bombers from the carriers took off and attacked the two cruisers, sinking both with a large loss of life. The cruiser HMS *Enterprise* and destroyers HMS *Paladin* and HMS *Panther* managed to rescue over 1,000 survivors who had spent many hours in the water.

The Japanese fleet then attacked Colombo with their carrier based aircraft on the 5th April 1942, damaging harbour installations, air bases and also anchored warships. As the 5th April was Easter Sunday, this became known as 'The Easter Sunday Raid'. A few days later the Japanese also made aircraft strikes on Trincomalee.

After the raids on Ceylon in April 1942 by the Japanese, the Royal Navy operations were mainly confined to the Indian Ocean and attacks in the Bay of Bengal. In the meantime the British Government was concentrating their armed forces on the war in Europe. It was left to the United States Navy (USN) to lead the resistance against the Imperial Japanese Navy (IJN) in the Pacific.

The Australian Government was aware that they could be invaded by the Japanese in 1942, and with the Royal Navy not in a position to help, they asked the United States for military assistance, and US bases were set up in Australia.

Following the Japanese incursions into the Indian Ocean, the British and American leadership became concerned that they would be allowed by the Vichy French, who controlled Madagascar, to use the island as a base for their submarines to have easy access to attack the allied shipping lanes around Africa.

Operation Ironclad was launched on 5th May 1942, to capture the port of Diego Suarez, Madagascar. HMS *Indomitable* had joined HMS *Illustrious* and other warships from the British Home Fleet, and the Eastern Fleet was to take part in the operation, which was to be commanded by Rear Admiral E. N. Syfret.

After capturing the port, the British thought that the whole island would surrender, but that was not to be and fighting continued until November 5th 1942, when the island was finally taken.

The role of the Japanese submarines

The Japanese were heavily reliant on ships for supply to the homeland, and for resupply to their military forces in the areas they had occupied. However, due to the size of the Pacific Ocean there was a need for the Japanese to have submarines that were long range and could stay at sea for many days, and to meet that need the Japanese built some of the largest submarines with the fastest underwater speeds used in the Second World War.

While the Allied submarines were focused on seeking out, attacking and sinking Japanese ships and shipping, the Imperial Japanese Navy submarines were varied in their use and included submarines that carried aircraft and also carried cargo and supplies. They built medium and long range submarines, midget submarines and the manned *Kaiten* submarines, which were effectively used as a suicide weapon near the end of the war.

Although early in the Pacific War the Japanese submarines did attack some merchant ships in the Indian and Pacific Oceans, the main difference in their use, compared with the Allied submarines, was that they concentrated on seeking out and attacking warships, rather than surface cargo ships. However, their torpedoes, contrary to the problems that the American submarines had with their torpedo exploders in the early part of the Pacific War, were by far superior and harder to detect.

The Japanese submarines did have moderate success in 1942, sinking some US carriers, destroyers and other warships, but with the increasing numbers of Allied submarines, combined with intelligence monitoring focusing on analysing and decoding Japanese and German radio traffic and the developing technologies, the Japanese began to lose many of their own warships and cargo ships. Many submarines were forced to become 'underwater cargo ships' carrying supplies to their starving land forces who were cut off in the Pacific islands, and also carrying cargo as part of the Yanagi missions to Europe. These missions were mainly for the carrying of goods and materials between Japan, Italy and Germany.

Success of Intelligence Monitoring

An example of how the intelligence monitoring of the Japanese and German radio messages succeeded occurred when the British submarine HMS *Taurus* was given essential information to detect and destroy the Japanese submarine *I-34*. This was the very first Japanese submarine to be sunk by a British submarine. *I-34* was a Type B submarine, built for speed and long range, and it carried a seaplane. The seaplane was in a hanger built into the conning tower and was launched by catapult. However, only 1 of the 20 Type B submarines built survived the war.

I-34 left Kure on the 13th October 1943, under the command of Commander Uri, to sail on a Yanagi mission carrying materials and goods to German occupied France. These were missions that had previously been carried out by cargo ships, but with the loss of many of these ships the Japanese resorted to using submarines. Two other submarines had already completed the voyage to France. However, the code breakers at Bletchley Park intercepted radio messages between Tokyo and Berlin about *I-34* and was able to decode these messages.

After arriving at the Seletar Naval Base, *I-34* took on board a cargo of tin, tungsten and raw rubber, and early in the morning on the 11th November, *I-34* departed Seletar for Penang. It was intended to refuel *I-34* in the Indian Ocean before the submarine entered the South Atlantic. Lt. Cdr. Mervyn R. G. Wingfield on the submarine HMS *Taurus* was alerted by the British code breakers about the Japanese submarine and was able to see *I-34* on the surface. He ordered six torpedoes to be fired, one of which sank the *I-34* off Penang.

CHAPTER 11

The Tide turns and Disaster Strikes!

The Battle of Midway in 4-7 June 1942 was a disaster for the Japanese when they lost many of their aircraft carriers and subsequently seriously weakened their Imperial Navy. Their losses included 3,057 killed; the aircraft carriers *Akagi*, *Kaga*, *Soryu*, *Hiryu* and the heavy cruiser *Mikuma* sunk, with the *Mogami* badly damaged. Both the cruisers *Chikuma* and *Tone* lost all their floatplanes. The US Pacific Fleet losses included 340 killed, aircraft carrier USS *Yorktown* and destroyer USS *Hammann* and 145 aircraft.

As a result of the losses at Midway the decision was made in July 1942 by the Japanese leadership to develop the land-based air force and reorganise the Combined Fleet with the aircraft carriers in the Third Fleet.

A further defeat after a long battle for Guadacanal ended when the Japanese left the island on February 7th, 1943. After their defeat at Guadacanal, the Japanese forces were becoming more and more demoralized.

Admiral Yamamoto's aim to boost the morale of the Japanese forces

In April 1943, in an attempt to boost their morale, Admiral Yamamoto left on an inspection tour of their bases in the South Pacific. However, the Americans were able to intercept and decode a message that informed them that Admiral Yamamoto was to visit the Solomon Islands on the 18th April, 1943. 'Operation Vengeance' was put into action to attack and shoot down Admiral Yamamoto's aircraft, a Mitsubishi 'Betty' bomber. Sixteen P-38 lightning fighters from the American 339 Fighter Squadron were dispatched to intercept and shoot down his plane. When they arrived at their targets, there were two 'Betty' bombers escorted by six Zero ('Zeke') fighters, with Admiral Yamamoto on board one 'Betty' and Admiral Ugaki in the other. Both 'Bettys' were shot down and Admiral Yamamoto was killed when his aircraft crashed into the jungle. Admiral Ugaki's aircraft was hit, caught fire and ditched in the sea. In his diary Admiral Ugaki describes how he managed to float to the surface and struggled to swim to shore with a broken right wrist. After Admiral Ugaki had recovered from his injuries he became Commander of the 1st Battleship Division and was in command during the Battle of Leyte Gulf in October 1944.

Admiral Yamamoto's position as Commander of the Japanese Combined Fleet was taken over by Admiral Koga, but he was not the same league as Admiral Yamamoto, nor did he have enough of the aircraft or carriers to successfully challenge the Allied Forces, and this was effectively the beginning of the end for the Imperial Japanese Navy carrier force. Admiral Koga was later killed at the end of March 1944, when the aircraft he was travelling in crashed after encountering a typhoon, and so another Commander for the Combined Fleet was needed. That Commander was to be Admiral Soemu Toyoda.

Build-up of British Fleet Aircraft Carriers

For the most of 1943 there were no British aircraft carriers available in the Indian Ocean and the British Eastern Fleet had to rely on land-based aircraft cover from India and Ceylon. That situation changed when HMS *Illustrious* left the UK in January 1944 for Trincomalee, Ceylon, to join the Eastern Fleet for deployment in the Indian Ocean. During late February and into March, HMS *Illustrious* took part in 'Operation Sleuth' which was to intercept German blockade runners sailing from the Far East to Europe. HMS *Illustrious* sailed from Trincomalee, Ceylon, with the light cruiser RNZN *Gambia,* destroyer HMS *Rotherham* and Dutch destroyer HNMS *Tjerke Hiddes,* and was later joined by the heavy cruiser HMS *Sussex* to the south west of the Cocoa Island, but no blockade runner was intercepted.

The US President Franklin D. Roosevelt had intimated to the British Prime Minister at the Casablanca Conference in January

1943 that as soon as they could spare an American aircraft carrier they would send one to help the British Eastern Fleet in the Indian Ocean. It was not until the 4th March 1944 that the carrier USS *Saratoga*, with three destroyer escorts, USS *Dunlap*, USS *Fanning* and USS *Cummings*, sailed from Majuro Atoll in the Marshall Islands to join the British Eastern Fleet.

On the 21st March 1944, HMS *Illustrious* and the battlecruiser HMS *Renown*, battleships HMS *Queen Elizabeth* and HMS *Valiant*, cruisers HMS *London*, HMS *Cumberland*, RNZN *Gambia* and HMS *Ceylon*, along with the cover of ten destroyers, sailed to meet the US Task Group 58.5. The US Task Group consisted of the aircraft carrier USS *Saratoga* accompanied by the destroyers USS *Dunlap*, USS *Cummings*, and USS *Fanning* which was joining Eastern Fleet for 'Operation Diplomat'. This was to be an Allied training exercise in the Bay of Bengal, to practice and coordinate British and US procedures for the forthcoming operations for the British Pacific Fleet and the US Fleet.

The US and British ships rendezvoused at sea on the 27th March 1944, and after arrival at Trincomalee, intensive training was carried out at sea with the British and US vessels, including deck landings trials, with USS *Saratoga* and their pilots sharing their combat experiences while flying against the Japanese with the British pilots. The combined British and US ships left with HMS *Illustrious* and USS *Saratoga* on 16th April 1944, to carry out strikes on Sabang Island, Sumatra, on the 19th April 1944, as part of 'Operation Cockpit'. This strike was requested by the United States to distract the Japanese attention away from their proposed attack on Hollandia, Papua New Guinea (now known as Jayapura city).

The aircraft on HMS *Illustrious* included Barracuda bombers and Corsair fighters, and on board USS *Saratoga* were Dauntless and Avenger bombers and Hellcats fighters. The Japanese were not expecting an attack and were caught by surprise with the Allied aircraft attacking Sabang harbour and nearby airfields, badly damaging buildings and power facilities, and sinking the minelayer *Hatsutaka* and cargo ships *Kunitsu Maru* and *Haruno Maru*. The strike was very successful and although aircraft were damaged by AA fire, just one pilot ditched in the sea and the rescue submarine HMS *Tactician* was on hand to rescue the pilot.

This successful raid was followed by 'Operation Transom', and before this operation HMS *Illustrious* had her Barracuda bombers replaced with the American Avenger torpedo bombers. This was to be a raid on the harbour and refineries at Surabaya, Java, along with USS *Saratoga* on the 17th May 1944. The aim was to destroy the harbour and Japanese shipping, harbour facilities and refineries. It proved to be a very successful raid in destroying the oil supplies that the Japanese relied upon, and also sank a large number of shipping. After this attack on the 18th May, USS *Saratoga* and the three US destroyers left the Eastern Fleet to return to operations in the Pacific, and then on to the USA for her crew to have a much need rest after nine months of combat.

In the Pacific the United States Navy had built up a strong presence, and the British Government, aware that British territories were being liberated by the US Navy, were also aware that it was important, both politically and militarily to become involved in the Pacific war against the Japanese forces. The British Government's aim was to have the British territories liberated by British forces, especially Hong Kong.

The Prime Minister, Winston Churchill, was given that opportunity after the successful D-Day landings in Normandy in June 1944, leading to the advance on Germany. He concluded that the time was now right to return the Royal Navy to the Far East, and at the second Quebec conference, in September 1944, Winston Churchill offered to the United States President Franklin D. Roosevelt to send a Royal Navy Fleet to engage in operations with the US Navy against the Japanese. The US President accepted the offer and the wheels were set in motion.

HMS *Indomitable* rejoins the British Eastern Fleet

After a further refit in the Norfolk Navy Yard, Virginia, from January to April 1944, HMS *Indomitable* returned to UK in May 1944, to embark aircraft. In June, HMS *Indomitable* with HMS *Victorious*, which had just had a refit, left the UK for Trincomalee, Ceylon (now Sri Lanka), where they joined the

British Eastern Fleet on July 5th, which was being prepared for operations against the Japanese.

Hellcat taking off for attack on Padang   Courtesy of Paul Whiteing

On 23rd August, as part of 'Operation Boomerang', the British Eastern Fleet provided air-sea rescue facilities during attacks by US Army aircraft on Sumatra, and on the 24th August, as part of 'Operation Banquet', HMS *Indomitable* and HMS *Victorious*, escorted by HMS *Howe*, took part in attacks on an airfield at Padang, Sumatra, and attacks on a cement works at Indaroeng and harbour at Emmahaven, Indonesia. They were also in action in September, with an attack by aircraft from each carrier on the important railway junction and repair yard at Sigli, Sumatra, and as part of 'Operation Light' for bombing and photographic reconnaissance of the Nicobar Islands. However, during Operation Light there was a mistaken 'friendly fire' attack on the submarine HMS *Spirit*, but fortunately there were no casualties.

To support the US invasions in the Battle of Leyte Gulf, the British Eastern Fleet was requested by the Americans to engage in a series of strikes on the Nicobar Islands with an aim to divert some Japanese forces away from their main attack on Leyte. Over the period of five days starting on the 15th October, HMS

Indomitable was with Task Group 63.3 as part of 'Operation Millet' during the US landings on Leyte.

Barracuda returning from attack on Car Nicobar airfield.
One of the rescue submarines can be seen below
Courtesy of Paul Whiteing

The main focus of Operation Millet was to attack the airstrip on the island of Car Nicobar. The ships that were involved in the operation were both fleet carriers HMS *Indomitable* and HMS *Victorious,* the battleship HMS *Howe*, battle-cruiser HMS *Renown*, a further three cruisers and eleven destroyers. Two submarines were available for the rescue of ditched airmen. On the 19th October, Corsairs and Hellcats from HMS *Victorious* and HMS *Indomitable* attacked the Car Nicobar airstrip, but were challenged by Japanese Oscars, of which they shot down seven, with a loss of one Hellcat and two Corsairs. Once the airstrip had been destroyed, the surface ships were used for bombardment of the shore installations.

The Battle of Leyte Gulf

The aim of the Battle of Leyte Gulf was to begin operations to liberate the Philippines, with the first landings to take place on Leyte by the American amphibious forces under the command of

General Douglas MacArthur, with support from the US 7th Fleet, that also contained units of the Royal Australian Navy, under the command Vice Admiral Thomas Kinkaid, and Admiral Halsey's 3rd Fleet, along with Vice Admiral Mitscher's Fast Carrier Task Force 38 (TF38).

One of the problems about this action was that there was no American naval commander in overall command. Admiral Kinkaid and his 7th Fleet came under MacArthur as Supreme Allied Commander Southwest Pacific, while Admiral Halsey's 3rd Fleet came under Admiral Nimitz as Commander-in-Chief Pacific Ocean Areas. This was to prove a serious problem through communication failures and especially as Admiral Toyoda had set a trap to draw Admiral Halsey's fleet away from the amphibious landings on Leyte, leaving it without cover and open to Japanese attack.

On the 17th October 1944, the American 6th Ranger Battalion landed on the Suluan Island at the mouth of Leyte Gulf, in preparation for the amphibious troops landing on the shores of Leyte. The landings began with a naval bombardment on the 19th October, which destroyed much of the Japanese defences on the beaches, and the next day the US amphibious troops landed on the beaches as the first stage to capturing the Philippine islands, which was strategically positioned between Japan and the countries it had occupied in Southeast Asia. In losing the Philippines, Japan would have its oil supply routes cut off, which would also deprive its armed forces of essential supplies.

The Imperial Japanese Navy (IJN) had expected an invasion in the Philippines and prepared with the Sho-Go operations plan for the mobilization of its remaining major naval vessels, with the aim of defeating the Allied forces of the United States and Australia. The operation would be the total commitment of the Japanese fleet.

Sho-Go Operations ('Victory Operations')

The Battle of the Philippine Sea in June 1944 was a disaster for Japanese naval air power, and this forced Admiral Toyoda, Commander of the Combined Fleet, to plan in advance four Sho-

Go ('Victory Operations') that were effectively to be major naval operations using surface ships. Sho-Go 1 was the defence of the Philippines, Sho-Go 2 was the defence of Formosa, Sho-Go 3 was the defence of the Islands of Honshu and Shikoko, and Sho-Go 4 was the defence of the northern island of Hokkaida. With the attack on Suluan Island on the 17th October, Admiral Toyoda ordered the start of the Sho-Go operations, aware that challenging the Americans with such a plan was likely to result in the destruction of one or more of its attacking fleets. It was a calculated risk, because if they lost the shipping lane to the south of the Philippines, used by the oil tankers to carry essential fuel supplies to Japan, their warships would have great difficulty in getting their fuel when in Japanese waters.

Sho-Go 1 Defence of the Philippines
Courtesy of Gordon Smith   www.naval-history.net

For Sho-Go 1, Admiral Toyoda, commander of the Japanese Combined Fleet, had mobilized most of the remaining navy vessels with the aim of defeating the Americans in their planned invasion of Leyte Gulf. The first engagement was the Battle of the Sibuyan Sea that lasted from October 23rd to 24th, followed by the Battle of the Surigao Strait and the Battle off Samer on the 25th October, when Admiral Kurita warships were forced to break away and retreat with many of the ships sunk.

The start of the kamikaze suicide attacks

It was at the Battle of Leyte Gulf that the shortage of pilots and aircraft was highlighted, and this led to the start of the kamikaze suicide attacks on Allied carriers and warships. Vice Admiral Takijiro Onishi arrived in Manila in the Philippines to assume command of the First Air Fleet on the 17th October 1944, the very day that the American 6th Ranger Battalion landed on the Suluan Island. He was an experienced veteran pilot who had assisted the late Admiral Yamamoto in development of the Japanese Air Arm.

When Vice Admiral Onishi landed at Manila, he was shocked to see just how few serviceable Zeke (Zero) fighter aircraft he had available for his use, but with repairs to Betty bombers he managed to double the final aircraft total.

Since the fall of Saipan, Vice Admiral Onishi had been campaigning for a change in air attacks, allowing for kamikaze suicide pilots to crash their aircraft on to the flight decks of the American carriers. With the huge losses of aircraft and experienced pilots, there was the urgent requirement for more pilots to be trained to fly the many high quality aircraft being built by the Japanese. Vice Admiral Onishi knew that with the loss of so many aircraft and trained pilots, the only way was to use the newly trained and inexperienced pilots for kamikaze missions, who would see it as an honour to sacrifice their lives for their emperor and country. By diving on a ship or aircraft carrier they would do far more damage than any other type of bombing.

In the Japanese language, 'kamikaze' is usually translated as 'divine wind', and originated as the name of major typhoons in the 13th century that dispersed Mongolian Invasion Fleets. The formal term used for aviator suicide attack units from the Imperial Japanese Navy was officially called 'divine wind special attack units'.

At the beginning of the Second World War, the Japanese had highly trained pilots with up to 800 flying hours, including wide combat experience, gained from their war against China and Russia, before the Pacific War. The surprise attack on the American fleet at Pearl Harbour demonstrated the combination of fighters taking off from aircraft carriers and initiating a deadly strike on the warships and harbour facilities. However, one serious omission by the Japanese military was that they did not have in place an effective pilot training plan, which would replace the highly experienced pilots that were lost in combat.

Vice Admiral Onishi had concluded that to be able to produce the number of pilots required, they would have to sacrifice the number of flying hours that had been given to a pre-war trainee pilot. This worked out to approximately a quarter of the flying hours that a carrier pilot had flown before the Pacific War. It was just a matter of giving them basic training, with no experience of aerobatics or air combat training, and trainee pilots were lucky if they managed over 100 flying hours before going into combat.

This was almost the opposite of the importance placed by the Americans and their Allies, who had high quality pilot training in place, ensuring that their trainee pilots had full basic, intermediate and advanced training, including training in carrier landings. It was constant practice and more practice when working up to the combat missions, and even in-between the missions the practice continued, keeping the pilots at top standard.

As the Pacific War continued, Japan's aircraft industry was still turning out new fighters, but with the continuing kamikaze suicide attacks causing further loss of aircraft and pilots, combined with the poorly trained replacement pilots and lack of fuel supplies, matters were becoming serious for the Japanese war effort.

With loss of their carrier force in the battle for the Philippines there was a change of attitude from the Japanese leadership. There was no shortage of young men who were willing to give their life to the Emperor and their nation, and so the Japanese commanders began to turn to other types of suicide units, including the 'Kaiten' ('Turning to the heavens') suicide submarines, the 'Ohka' ('Cherry Blossom'), a kamikaze rocket plane, the 'Shinyo' ('Sea Quake') suicide boats, and the 'Fukuryu' ('Crouching Dragons') suicide divers.

When 857 Squadron arrived in Ceylon in October 1944, they would be facing an enemy whose aircraft attack tactics had developed into kamikaze suicide attacks on the carriers, flown by pilots that were willing to give their life for their emperor and nation.

CHAPTER 12

857 Squadron goes to War

HMS *Rajah* sailed from Belfast on the 10th September 1944 for Ceylon (Sri Lanka), calling at Gibraltar, Alexandria, Bombay and Aden, before their first disembarkations at Cochin, South India, on the 9th October, and then on to Colombo.

857 Squadron at Katakarunda. Sub. Lt. Wright is fourth from the left in the second row.
Geoffrey Wright Collection

Members of 857 Squadron disembarked and were taken to RNAS Katukurunda (HMS Ukassa), where they were to live in thatched huts and had the task of getting used to the snakes, scorpions, and the monkeys that kept an eye on them. A great pleasure was the food they received in the mess, where they were able to have salads and cold meat or very tasty curry.

HMS *Rajah* continued on to Trincomalee, arriving on October

11th when the Avengers were unloaded and a team of pilots started to ferry the aircraft down to RNAS Katakurunda, landing on the metal runway which was laid out in a jungle clearing.

Katakurunda   *Courtesy of Paul Whiteing*

After arrival in Ceylon, the first entries recorded in Sub. Lt. Wright's logbook start on the 12th November, when Sub. Lt. Braithwaite flew with Sub. Lt. Wright in TBM JZ432 to assist him familiarise himself with the local area, including 6 plane formations and 6 ADDLs (Aerodrome Dummy Deck Landings).

On the 14th November he was joined by his air gunner, while he practised more ADDLs. For the following days it was mainly practice with his aircrew, Sub. Lt. Glendinning and L/A Slight, for high level glide bombing on towed target, and turret firing.

On the 22 November 1944 the British Pacific Fleet (BPF) was formed under Admiral Sir Bruce Fraser, who was the Commander of the British Eastern Fleet from August 1944, and then Commander-in-Chief of the British Pacific Fleet. HMS *Indomitable,* HMS *Illustrious* and HMS *Victorious* of the 1st Aircraft Carrier Squadron, and other fleet vessels became part of British Pacific Fleet, which was to be based in Trincomalee, Ceylon.

The fourth aircraft carrier to join the British Pacific Fleet was HMS *Indefatigable*, which was commissioned into the Royal Navy on 3rd May 1944. She joined the Home Fleet and took part in raids on the German battleship *Tirpitz* in the Norway Fjords, and then went into the dockyard for work, before sailing on the 19th November for the Far East to join the Pacific Fleet, arriving on the 10th December at Colombo carrying the Avengers of 820 Squadron.

Admiral Lord Louis Mountbatten, Supreme Allied Commander Southeast Asia Command (SEAC) 1943-46, with Captain Eccles on a visit to HMS Indomitable.

Also serving with the BPF, on the destroyer HMS Whelp, was Lt. Philip Mountbatten, who is now Prince Philip, Duke of Edinburgh.

Frank Stockwell Collection – courtesy of Emma Stockwell www.maritimequest.com

The British Pacific Fleet was a multi-national fleet and although the majority was Royal Navy ships, there were ships from the Royal Australian Navy (RAN), Royal New Zealand Navy (RNZN) and the Royal Canadian Navy (RCN).

On the day that the British Pacific Fleet was formed, Sub. Lt. Wright was flying in JZ564 with L/A Slight and L/A Pettit for practice on air to sea turret firing, followed the next day in JZ426 with his aircrew for over sea navex (navigation exercises), but had to return because of bad weather.

Operation Outflank

Operation Outflank was a series of operations against the oil installations on Sumatra. The first series was attacks on the oil installations in northern Sumatra as part of 'Operation Robson' and 'Operation Lentil', and the attacks on the oil installations in southern Sumatra as part of 'Operation Meridian 1 and 2', while the British Pacific Fleet was en-route to Australia in January 1945.

Force 67, under the overall command of Rear-Admiral Vian, left Trincomalee on the 17th November 1944, to carry out air attacks on oil installations on Pangkalan Brandan. Aircraft carriers HMS *Indomitable* and HMS *Illustrious* sailed with the cruisers HMS *Newcastle*, HMS *Argonaut* and HMS *Black Prince* under the protection of the destroyers HMS *Kempenfelt*, HMS *Whirlwind*, HMS *Wrangler*, HMS *Wessex* and HMS *Wakeful*. Refuelling was provided by Force 69, with the tanker RFA *Wave King* under the escort of the destroyers HMS *Whelp* and HMS *Wager* on the 18th November.

The strike force was in position by November 20th 1944, but despite the weather conditions being poor, the final decision to take off was made by Rear-Admiral Vain. Aircraft taking part in the strike consisted of 12 Avengers (one crashing on take-off) from HMS *Indomitable*, and 16 Avengers from HMS *Illustrious*, each carrying 4 x 500lb bombs, and 4 Corsairs from HMS *Illustrious* each carrying 2 x 500lb bombs. Air cover was provided by 8 Hellcats (Top Cover) and 8 Hellcats (Close Cover) from HMS *Indomitable*, 12 Corsairs (Middle Cover) from HMS *Illustrious* and 8 Hellcats from HMS *Indomitable*.

However, the weather over the target was poor and this forced a change of plan to air attacks on the oil installations at Belawan Deli, Sumatra, and a further attack on the Sabang airfield by 8 Hellcats from HMS *Indomitable* and 8 Corsairs from HMS *Illustrious*. Apart from the shooting down of one Japanese Sally (Mitsubishi Ki-21 bomber) there were no losses to the British aircraft.

When referring to the names of the attacking Japanese aircraft the Americans had developed a code of names to distinguish the aircraft. These were mainly boy's names for the fighters and girl's names for the bombers, and this code was adopted by the British. For example a 'Zeke' referred to a Mitsubishi A6M Zero and an 'Oscar' was the Nakajima Ki-43 Hayabusa ('Hayabusa' meaning 'Peregrine Falcon').

It was on the 27th November 1944, that Sub. Lt. Wright finally joined HMS *Indomitable* when he flew solo in JZ424 from the land base to the carrier for deck landing training. On the next day he flew with Sub. Lt. Glendinning and L/A Slight for formation flying and high altitude bombing on a towed target. Later that day flying with his aircrew in JZ565 for over sea navex, he recorded in his logbook 'Successful!!!'

The aircrews' practice for combat was ceaseless to ensure that by the time they took part in strikes many of the skills would come as second nature, allowing for reaction against the unexpected situations that they had not experienced before.

December started for Sub. Lt. Wright with plenty of practice in formation flying, fighter evasion and glide bombing, but on the 7th December there was practice in accelerated take-offs and further dive bombing attacks, until the 13th December when, with his aircrew in JZ567, he took part in 8 dive bombing attacks on a fixed target at China Bay, which was land based.

Just a few days later 857 Squadron was to leave on HMS *Indomitable* for their first strike on Japanese targets in Sumatra, but not all the 857 Squadron Avengers were selected to take part in this strike as part of 'Operation Robson'.

Operation Robson, Northern Sumatra

There was a further air attack on Belawan Deli by aircraft from HMS *Indomitable* (Flag: Rear Admiral Aircraft Carriers BPF) and HMS *Illustrious*. The aircraft on board the carriers for this strike consisted of:

HMS *Illustrious*: 1830 Squadron (Lt. Cdr. Tritton) 18 Corsair II, 1833 Squadron (Lt. Cdr. Hanson) 18 Corsair II, 854 Squadron (Lt. Cdr. Mainprice) 21 Avenger II

HMS *Indomitable*: 1839 Squadron (Lt. Cdr. Shotton) 15 Hellcat I, 1844 Squadron (Lt. Cdr. Godson) 14 Hellcat I, 857 Squadron (Lt. Cdr. Stuart) 21 Avenger II

HMS *Illustrious* and HMS *Indomitable* were escorted by HMS *Newcastle* from the East Indies Fleet, along with cruisers HMS *Black Prince* and Argonaut, and 7 destroyers of the 27th Destroyer Flotilla left Trincomalee on the 17th December for a strike on airfields in the Sabang area and targets at Belawan Deli, which took place on the 20th December as part of Operation Robson. This was not very successful and the fleet returned to base on the 22nd December.

For Sub. Lt. Wright and his aircrew it was their final preparation before going into combat. On the 21st December, flying Avenger JZ588, Sub. Lt. Wright and his crew acted as a target plane for three cruisers, consisting of straight attacks from 3,000ft and 200ft. They also did a radar calibration for HMS *Indomitable*, although the radar on the aircraft was not as good as that on the carrier. On board JZ588 that day was a US Army photographer.

Sub. Lt. Wright flew from China Bay to RNAS Katakarunda on the 27th December in Avenger JZ424. RNAS Katakarunda (HMS *Ukussa*) was also used for jungle training, because of the jungle terrain. He landed on the airstrip cut out of an area of jungle and laid with metal matting and returned later that day.

The next day Sub. Lt. Wright flew with a passenger to HMS *Indefatigable* and returned to HMS *Indomitable* with dispatches.

On December 29th there was a full-scale practice bombing attack on China Bay with TBM Avengers, F6F Hellcats, F4U Corsairs, Fairey Fireflies and Supermarine Seafires from three aircraft carriers. The next day Sub. Lt. Wright, along with his navigator Sub. Lt. Glendinning, ferried three pilots, Sub. Lts. Dee, Adam and Langshaw, in Avenger JZ424 from China Bay to Katakarunda, when they would fly three Avengers in formation back to HMS *Indomitable* the same day.

This was to be the end of the training and practice for Sub. Lt. Wright and his crew prior to going into combat. However, consistent practice sessions were always ongoing to keep the pilots and their crew at their peak performance, rather than getting bored and their attack and evasion skills standard dropping, thus causing more casualties.

The logbook was signed off by Sub. Lt. Wright on the 31st December 1944, and it recorded that Sub. Lt. Wright had completed 464hrs 15mins flying hours. It was checked and signed by Lt. Morris Senior Pilot, and stamped by the Commanding Officer 857 Squadron Lt. Cdr. (Doc) Stuart.

CHAPTER 13

Operation Lentil

The oil refineries in Sumatra were essential to the Japanese war effort because they eliminated the problem of having to transport crude oil by sea to Japan for refining. Therefore the oil refineries at Pangkalan Brandan, a port town in northern Sumatra, and Palembang, in southern Sumatra, which produced 50% of oil and 75% of the aviation spirit used by Japan, were important targets for the British Pacific Fleet.

The British Pacific Fleet Task Force 65 left Trincomalee on the 1st January 1945, to engage in the carrier-borne aircraft attacks on the Pangkalan Brandan as part of 'Operation Lentil'. The aim was to attack the oil refineries at Pangkalan Brandan, Sumatra, and this strike was supervised by the newly appointed British Pacific Fleet's Air Co-ordinator Commander, Ronald Hay R.M.

Task Force 65 consisted of the aircraft carriers:

HMS *Indomitable* with 857 Squadron (Lt. Cdr. Stuart) Avengers, 1839 (Lt. Cdr. Shotton) and 1844 (Lt. Cdr. Godson) Squadrons Hellcats)

HMS *Victorious* with 849 Squadron (Lt. Cdr. Foster) Avengers, 1834 (Lt. Cdr. Hopkins) and 1836 (Lt. Cdr. Tomkinson) Squadrons Corsairs)

HMS *Indefatigable* with 820 Squadron (Lt. Cdr. Luke) Avengers 887 (Lt. Cdr. Thomson) and 894 (Lt. Cdr. Crossman) Squadrons Seafires and 1770 Squadron (Major Cheesman) Fireflies).

For the Operation Lentil, 888 Squadron (Lt. Cdr. Mann) Hellcat PR II embarked on HMS *Indefatigable* for specialised PR (Photographic Reconnaissance) work. These Hellcats had the designation 'Hellcat PR II' because they were unarmed, but if they were armed their designation would have been 'Hellcat FR II'.

The carriers were escorted by the cruisers HMS *Suffolk*, HMS *Ceylon*, HMS *Argonaut* and HMS *Black Prince*, and protected by the destroyers HMS *Kempenfelt,* HMS *Whelp*, HMS *Grenville*, HMS *Wager*, HMS *Urania*, HMS *Undaunted,* HMS *Undine* and HMS *Ursa.*

At first light the carrier crews were manning their stations, while the pilots and their crews were below decks having their early breakfast. The engines of the aircraft were being warmed up and the carriers started to prepare by turning into the wind for the first planes to take off. When the Ramrod (low-level attacks against ground targets) fighters had left to attack and strafe the Japanese airfields, the Avengers took off and climbed to over 10,000ft in order to cross the range of mountains on the Sumatra coastline.

The attacks successfully took place on the 4th January, with Ramrod attacks by fighters on nearby airfields destroying aircraft on the ground, while making it safer for the Firefly rocket attacks, and the Avengers bombing while having CAP (Combat Air Patrol) by the fighters. The strike aircraft consisted of 16 Avengers from 857 Squadron on HMS *Indomitable* and 16 Avengers from 849 Squadron on HMS *Victorious*, each carrying 4 x 500lb bombs. There were 12 Fireflies from HMS Indefatigable, armed with 8 x 60lb rockets, 8 Hellcats (Top Cover) from HMS *Indomitable,* 16 Corsairs (Middle Cover) from HMS *Victorious,* 8 Hellcats (Close Cover) from HMS *Indomitable,* with the CAP shooting down 5 Japanese Oscars.

To take out ground targets, there were the fighter Ramrods attacks of 8 Hellcats from HMS *Indomitable* and 8 Corsairs from HMS *Victorious*, which successfully destroyed seven aircraft on the ground and shot down one Sally and one Dinah. Photo Reconnaissance was carried out by a detachment of 8 Hellcats from 888 Squadron on HMS *Indefatigable.*

Damage inflicted on the refinery indicated one tanker and also two railway engines hit, as well as the shooting down of Japanese aircraft. The British loss was one Avenger damaged by a Japanese fighter, one Avenger that had to ditch with engine failure and a

Firefly that ran out of fuel, but the crews were rescued. Force 63 then set sail to return to Trincomalee, arriving on the 7th January.

Avenger 377 flown by Sub. Lt. (A) Geoffrey Wright RNVR in attack on Pangkalan Brandan.   Geoffrey Wright Collection

Sub. Lt. Wright took part in the Avenger squadron attack on the oil refineries at Pangkalan Brandan and felt very lucky that he and his crew survived their first encounters with the Japanese:

'There were quite a few of us sharing a cabin and in advance of a strike, the steward would come in to wake us up. He would say, 'It is 04.00hrs sir, and you are on the next strike.' As each pilot was woken up, there were many groans. We would get ready and go to breakfast, which was a jolly good meal, but most of us couldn't eat, because we were feeling quite nervous about the strike.

The briefing before attack was held in the briefing room by the Naval Commander in charge. Detailed models of the refineries were on display, which helped the briefing officer to explain to the aircrew on individual or specific targets and for us to have a better idea of what the target looked like. The briefing officer would inform us what we could expect when we arrived over the target, but they would let you know as little as possible. That was because if you were shot down and captured by the Japanese, they would first torture you for information and then execute you. We had been given advance warning that any pilots captured would be tortured before execution by decapitation.

Then we went to our planes, which were lined up on the flight deck, and took off at 15 second intervals. The 2 squadrons of Hellcat fighters would usually take off first and our squadron of Avengers would then take off and join up with the fighters overhead. There was always one big problem which happened every time we took off and that was being fired at by our own ships. Often this would resort to the CO transmitting to the ships, 'Would you kindly stop shooting at us.'

Attacking Pangkalan Brandan refinery.
Courtesy of Paul Whiteing

'I was flying the TBM Avenger JZ434 with Sub. Lt. Glendinning and L/A Slight as crew when we attacked the oil refinery at Pankalan Brandan dropping 4-500lb M.C. Bombs. The action of the aircraft from HMS *Indomitable* was for our Avenger bombers and two squadrons of Hellcats flying in tight formation with the Avengers to protect them from attack by Japanese aircraft. It took us two hours to reach the target.

We were always attacked by Japanese fighters and the nearest I got to being shot down was when the Avenger flying alongside me got hit and I saw black holes appearing across his wing where a Jap fighter had hit him. I thought I was to be next, but one of our fighters shot the Jap fighter down.

We were in V formations and when we arrived over the target the CO leading the attack indicated with hand on top of head and pointed either to L or R side and broke silence with 'GO, GO, GO!' Away went No 1, No 2 and No 3, at 25 sec intervals. We flew straight down, almost vertically, to attack the target with AA (Anti-Aircraft) firing and the orange tracer coming up towards us, and also there was the black flak. The feeling at first was of being very scared, with black explosions of shells off your wings and to the side, but you soon forgot it and concentrated on what you had to do.

We dropped our bombs on our set target, which we had seen on the model of refinery on board in the briefing room, but the only one who would see if we hit the target was the tail gunner. We then followed a river just 20ft off the water while swaying side to side, passing a little island, and then I pulled back the stick. It was then you felt very lonesome, just then over the sea looking for your formation so you could rendezvous and then fly back to HMS *Indomitable*.

The CO was always first to land, and then the rest of the squadron landed in turn. Sometimes the Hellcats may be short of fuel and would have to land first.

When you had landed, the crash barrier would go down and you would go over it. On the aircraft carrier there were two hangers, one on top of the other. The wings were folded on the Avenger, you switch off, and then the aircraft is pulled in to park on deck.

857 Squadron Commanding Officer Lt. Cdr. (Doc) Stuart
first one to land back on HMS Indomitable after completing the mission.
Frank Stockwell Collection courtesy of Emma Stockwell www.maritimequest.com

'After you returned there was the debriefing, generally to get information on all that had happened. It was then that we got to know if anyone was lost. It was always very sad when we lost some of our colleagues, because it would then mean new pilots joining the squadron.

After the debriefing, we would go and wash and shower and then have something to eat before going for a sleep in your pit. That may not always be possible because we may have two flights in a day, one in the morning and one in the afternoon. Sometimes we would have a good old sing-song for relaxation.

Avenger 378 catches wire safely and lands on HMS Indomitable
Frank Stockwell Collection

114

'After we had returned to our base, I was again in the air on the 6th January with my aircrew for radar calibration, and on the 12th January in Avenger JZ372, I flew Sub. Lt. Staniforth from Katakarunda to China Bay for ferrying aircraft so that all carriers were fully equipped for our forthcoming operations.'

Avenger 372 Lands safely on HMS Indomitable.
Frank Stockwell Collection

Following the early operations against the Sumatra oil refineries in November and December 1944, and then the attack on Pangkalan Brandan in early January, there was intense training and equipping of the air squadrons for their next operation, which was to be 'Operation Meridian'. A rehearsal for Operation Meridian was carried out on the 13th January, and the outcome was that the Task Force was ready to undertake such an important attack against the Japanese oil industry in Sumatra.

Sub. Lt. Wright and his crew were to take part in this rehearsal:

'On the 13th January I flew with my aircrew, Sub. Lt. Glendinning and L/A Slight, in Avenger JZ424 as part of a large scale practice for our next mission. This was a three hour practice strike on Colombo, but that evening after I had landed back on board HMS *Indomitable* I was very tired and decided to go to have a shower. I tripped up on the way to the bathroom, sustaining some quite serious injuries, but stayed on board HMS *Indomitable* while recovering from the injury. I had been taken off flying duty, and during the interim became a desk officer with the job of issuing pilots with their aircraft.'

While off flying duty, Sub. Lt. Wright had taken over a role as desk officer, allocating planes to the pilots for missions, but one thing that has always haunted him was the loss of the Squadron Leader of the fighters:

'The problem arose after I had allocated all the aircraft to all the fighter pilots. I had allocated a particular aircraft to the Squadron Leader and he was not happy with it because he said it was a terribly slow fighter. He pleaded with me to change the aircraft, but I was in a difficult position because I had already allocated all the aircraft. The Squadron Leader became angry, and although my rank was Sub. Lt. and I was junior to the Squadron Leader, he had to accept the aircraft allocated to him. I told him that my job was to allocate the aircraft and that all had been allocated to pilots and that there were no spare aircraft. The Squadron Leader said that if he flew the aircraft it would kill him, as its performance was so bad. It was an impossible situation for me as I could not take an aircraft back from another pilot, and in the end the Squadron Leader had to accept the allocated airplane. I felt terrible, because he did not come back from the mission, but I recognised that it was wartime and that the plane had to be used by a pilot and I had no other choice.'

CHAPTER 14

British Pacific Fleet transfers its base to Sydney, Australia, in 1945

Task Force 63

Task Force 63 included four aircraft carriers, HMS *Indomitable*, Captain J. A. S. Eccles and Flagship of Rear Admiral Sir Philip Louis Vian, HMS *Victorious*, Captain M. M. Denny, HMS *Indefatigable*, Captain Q. D. Graham, HMS *Illustrious*, Captain C. E. Lambe, the Battleship HMS *King George V* (Flag Vice Admiral Sir Henry Bernard Rawlings 2nd in Charge, British Pacific Fleet), Captain B. B. Schofield, with the cruisers HMS *Black Prince*, HMS *Argonaut,* HMS *Ceylon* and HMS *Euryalus*, and destroyers HMS *Grenville* (D25), HMS *Undainted*, HMS *Undine*, HMS *Ursa,* HMS *Kempenfelt* (D27), HMS *Wager*, HMS *Wakeful,* HMS *Whelp* and HMS *Whirlwind*.

The British Pacific Fleet left Trincomalee at 14.30 hours as Task Force 63, on Tuesday, 16th January 1945, for further operations in the Indian Ocean, prior to transferring its operations to a main base to be established in Sydney, with an intermediate base at Manus Island in the Bismarck Archipelago, the largest of the 18 Admiralty Islands.

The light cruiser HMS *Ceylon* and destroyer HMS *Wessex* remained in Trincomalee to embark mail and spares before sailing a little later. The Refuelling Group Task Force 69 had already sailed in advance of the main fleet on Saturday, 13th January, to be in position for the refuelling operations.

Operation Meridian One

The aim of the operation against the two oil refineries at Songei Gerong and Pladjoe, in Sumatra, was the destruction of these oil plants to deny the Japanese the fuel and oil supplies they relied so heavily upon for their warfare operations.

Whilst en route to Sumatra, the fleet practised various exercises and manoeuvres, including gunnery and torpedo attacks, until meeting the Task Force 69, consisting of the RFA oil tankers, *Echodale*, *Wave King* and *Empire Savage*, under the protection of the destroyer HMS *Urchin*, for refuelling. The refuelling group was not at the rendezvous position when Task Force 63 arrived, but an aircraft search located Task Force 69 and once in position refuelling began. Due to the poor weather conditions it was not easy to accomplish the refuelling and damage to the oiling equipment was caused by the destroyers. The time taken in refuelling and also the weather conditions while sailing to the flying off positions, held back the planned attacks. During the passage to the flying off point, Rear Admiral Vian was required to take over operational command of Task Force 63, due to Vice Admiral Rawlings falling ill.

With better conditions prevailing, Task Force made its final approach to the flying off position during the night of the 23rd/24th January. By dawn the weather was clear and fine and importantly, the mountains that the aircraft had to fly over could be clearly seen in the distance.

On the 24th January 1945, aircraft from the British Pacific Fleet, under the command of Rear Admiral Vain, were in position to successfully attack the large oil installations at Pladjoe, Palembang, Sumatra, and the Royal Dutch Shell refinery, as part of Operation Meridian One. The Air Coordinator was Major Hay RM, who was to fly in an Avenger with the attack force.

The targets were surrounded by jungle and a river running inland and past the refinery, where tankers were able to dock. Advance reconnaissance reports from US aircraft indicated a heavy defensive AA (Anti-Aircraft) and fighter aircraft in a ring of airfields around the target.

The aircraft on board each aircraft carrier for the Pladjoe strike consisted of:

HMS *Indomitable*: 857 Squadron (Lt. Cdr. Stuart) (21 Avenger II) and 1839 (Lt. Cdr. Shotton) squadron (15 Hellcats), 1844 Squadron (Lt. Cdr. Godson) (14 Hellcats I).

HMS *Indefatigable*: 820 Squadron (Lt. Cdr. Luke) (21 Avenger II), 1770 Squadron (Majot Cheesman) (12 Firefly I) and 887 Squadron (Lt. Cdr. Thomson) (24 Seafires) and 894 Squadron (Lt Cdr Crossman) (16 Seafires).

HMS *Victorious*: 849 Squadron (Lt. Cdr. Foster) (21 Avenger II) 1834 Squadron (Lt. Cdr. Hopkins) (18 Corsair II) and 1836 Squadron (Lt. Cdr. Tomkinson) (16 Corsair (II) and the ships flight of 2 Walrus Amphibian Detachment for ASR (Air Sea Rescue).

HMS *Illustrious*: 854 Squadron (Lt. Cdr. Mainprice) (21 Avengers I and II) 1830 Squadron (Lt. Cdr. Trotton) (16 Corsairs II) and 1833 Squadron (Lt. Cdr. Hanson) (16 Corsairs II).

The Pladjoe Refinery Strike Force

'Strike One Wing' consisted of 12 Avengers (857 Squadron) and 16 Hellcats (Close Cover) from HMS *Indomitable*, and 12 Avengers (849 Squadron) and 16 Corsairs (Top Cover) from HMS *Victorious*. The strike leader was Lt. Col. Stuart RNVR, who was the CO of 857 Squadron.

'Strike Two Wing' consisted of 12 Avengers (854 Squadron) and 8 Corsairs (Middle Cover) from HMS *Illustrious*, and 12 Avengers (820 Squadron) from HMS *Indefatigable*. Each Avenger carried 4 x 500lb bombs.

'Strike and Escort' consisted of 12 Fireflies from HMS *Indefatigable* each armed with 60lb rockets.

'Strike on Mana airfield' consisted of 4 Avengers and 4 Hellcats from HMS *Indomitable*.

'The Ramrod Sweeps' by fighters to destroy ground targets over the Japanese Airfields, were 12 Corsairs from HMS *Victorious* and 12 Corsairs from HMS *Illustrious*. PR (Photographic Reconnaissance) was undertaken by 2 Hellcats from HMS *Indomitable* and ASR (Air-Sea-Rescue) by 2 Supermarine Walrus amphibians (Darby and Joan) from HMS *Victorious*.

The Japanese Air Defence of Sumatra in January 1945 was the 9th Air Division of 7th Army fighter squadrons from the 21st, 26th,

33rd, 87th, and Air Regiments 24th and 71st Independent Air Squadrons and the 74th Air Recce Squadron. The 58th Air Regiment was also based in Sumatra. Four of the fighter squadrons were based on the airfields around Palembang.

The first strike aircraft began taking off from the carriers at 06.15 hours from a flying off position some seventy miles east of Engano Island. Once all aircraft had been assembled, the strike force, consisting of Avengers carrying 4 x 500lb bombs and including rocket firing Fireflies, Corsairs and Hellcats fighters for CAP (Combat Air Patrol), left for their strike on Pladjoe refinery. At the same time, the Mana airfield strike left for its target area.

There were some problems in getting all the aircraft in the air, and this caused the Fireflies to have to catch up with their main strike force. However, the fighter sweep of Corsairs was able to overtake the strike force and started its sweep on Lembak airfield, to the surprise of the Japanese.

7P Avenger taking off, but this aircraft is thought to have been shot down over Palembang.   *Frank Stockwell Collection*

The Japanese fighter airfields situated around Palembang, southern Sumatra, were to protect the area against an Allied attack, especially on the Pladjoe refinery. The Palembang P2

120

airfield was not discovered by the Japanese until the 21 February 1942, with the first aircraft arriving three days later. The main Sentai (Squadron) using the base was the 87th Sentai of the IJAAF (Imperial Japanese Army Air Force).

For the 87th Sentai it was a very quiet posting and up until then they had no combat experience.

IJAAF Army Ki-44 'Tojo' Courtesy of Ray Crupi

That was until the 24th January 1945, when British Corsairs and Hellcats did a Ramrod sweep of the airfield destroying a large number of their Nakajima Ki-44 (Tojo's) on the ground. However, at the time a flight of Tojos were waiting to take off, led by Captain Hideaki Inayama, a Japanese ace.

Although some of the aircraft lined up for take off were hit and seriously damaged, Captain Inayama managed to take off and was successful in shooting down two Avengers. The total loss to the 87th Sentai was twelve aircraft and seven pilots, but the attacks on the 24th and 29th January 1942 were the only actions the 87th Sentai had experienced.

When the strike aircraft arrived at Palembang, the Japanese were ready for them with very accurate flak defences. Despite the intensity of the flak, the Ramrod sweeps still destroyed 34 aircraft on the ground and damaged many more, seriously affecting the Japanese getting aircraft in the air to attack the strike force, and importantly, protecting the oil refineries.

Once the strike force made landfall, they had to climb to 7,000 feet to clear the Barisan Mountains. As the Avenger approached the target, the strike leaders of each strike force prepared their group for attack by sending them into line astern formation, and then giving the 'GO' when their turn came. The Avengers would then start their glide bombing run from approximately 10,000ft, but soon found the defence was fierce with Anti-Aircraft fire bursting at different heights, and the attacks by the enemy fighters, as well as the cover aircraft getting into dog fights with the Japanese aircraft. Lt. Cdr. David Foster, Commander of 849 Squadron, describes the scene where the sky was filled with fighters:

> 'Theirs and ours, screaming like disturbed gulls, heavy ack-ack bursting around us and the radio waves filled with shouted warnings.'

A complete surprise for the pilots was the barrage balloons that were released just as the attack began. These barrage balloons had not been identified in advance by the reconnaissance aircraft and needed quick thinking by each pilot to avoid the wires, as well as judging where the wires were in relation each balloon.

Bombing Palembang   Frank Stockwell Collection

If the pilot was lucky enough to see the wires and avoid them, he could press home his attack, but if not, then he could have his wings sliced off, causing him to crash. At first the balloons were flying at approximately 2,000 feet, but as the strike force of Avengers and Fireflies arrived at the target, the balloons were raised at varying heights up to 4,000 feet. Quite a number of Avenger pilots decided to dive through the balloons to press home their attack. Although it was almost impossible to see the wires, they still took the risk to ensure they hit their set targets.

There was a group of Tojo and Nick fighters which attacked the escorts about 15 miles from the target, but as they made an attempt to attack the strike force, the escort fighters dealt with them. Other aircraft were destroyed on the ground through the Ramrod attacks.

By 09.00 hours the Avengers had dropped their bombs and had headed for their rendezvous, approximately 30 miles away, after passing over intense flak near the town of Palembang. Once assembled they would head for the Task Force position, and by 10.30 hours all aircraft had landed back on the carriers, with the exception of two Avengers, one Hellcat and six Corsairs, which failed to return. It was thought that some crews may have landed safely, but had been taken prisoner. Other losses included one Corsair and one Seafire, whose pilots had managed to make it back to the fleet, before bailing out into the sea and being rescued.

Sub. Lt. (A) Frank Stovin-Bradford RNVR was part of the small strike force sent to Mana airfield, and from approximately 8,000ft the 4 Avengers split into pairs and attacked the two parallel runways, which they cratered, while the 4 Hellcat fighters strafed the aircraft on the ground, managing to destroy one aircraft. Although there was AA defensive fire, there seemed to be very little going on. One Hellcat pilot was injured by the AA fire, but was able to fly safely back to HMS *Indomitable*.

The pilots had been prepared well in advance of the strikes in the briefing rooms on board the carriers, where accurate scale models of the targets and maps were available to gain a clear picture of the area. This was important for them to know if they were shot down by enemy aircraft or anti-aircraft fire while over land. For those pilots who were forced to bail out and parachute safely to the ground, they would need to try to make their way across country to the south coast where the rescue submarines would have been waiting for some days and nights after the attack to pick up any airman who had ditched in the sea, or had escaped through the jungle and mountains while avoiding Japanese troops and had safely reached the coast. As well as the submarines, the fleet's two Walrus amphibians, which were known as 'Darby and Joan', were in the air searching for ditched airman, but none were sighted.

The pilots were prepared for any eventualities and were dressed in khaki trousers and shirts, containing maps, gold coins to bribe any natives into helping them if they came down in the jungle, and for protection, a commando knife and revolver. Over their clothes they wore a Mae West, which contained an escape kit and other equipment in case they ditched in the sea. Importantly, no other identification, apart from their dog tag that gave name and number around their neck, but no indication of their rank. This was especially important, because the Japanese had clearly warned that any officer pilot who was captured would be interrogated, before being executed by beheading.

Photographic Reconnaissance revealed that there were hits on a number of the set targets at the Pladjoe refinery, and included a radio station which was hit while the aircraft were leaving the target area for their rendezvous. The fighter escorts had claimed to have shot down at least 13 fighters and this was very close to the Japanese broadcast that confirmed they had lost 14 aircraft, which included Tojos, Oscars and twin-engined Nicks.

The Task Force then left the area to engage in further refuelling on the 26th and 27th January. After the refuelling was completed, the Task Force returned to the flying off area on the 29th January, for the aircraft to take off for one more attack on the oil installations at Soengei Gerong, the East Indies oil refinery for the Standard Oil Company, and airfields surrounding the plant, as part of 'Operation Meridian Two'.

Operation Meridian Two

One of the concerns in the planning of the second attack on the Soengei Gerong oil refinery was that the Japanese would already be alert after the attack on Pladjoe refinery, and in addition any captured pilots and aircrew would possibly have been tortured for information. They would be expecting a further attack on the Songei Gerong refinery and would be ready. The two wing leaders were also concerned about the heavy concentration of AA fire around the town of Palembang, which the first strike aircraft experienced when they flew over when making for the rendezvous. For the second strike the aircraft would be instructed to turn right after they had dropped their bombs, passing south of the target. The other concern was that the Japanese would possibly make an attempt to attack the Fleet with their fighter force.

The aircraft to be used on the Songei Gerong strike included:

HMS *Indomitable*: 12 Avengers, 16 Hellcats (Middle Cover)

HMS *Illustrious*: 12 Avengers, 12 Corsairs (Top Cover)

HMS *Victorious*: 12 Avengers, 12 Corsairs (Close Cover)

HMS *Indefatigable*: 12 Avengers, 12 Fireflies.

For the Fighter Ramrod Sweeps:

HMS *Illustrious*: 12 Corsairs concentrating on Lembak Airfield

HMS *Victorious*: 12 Corsairs concentrating on Talanbetoetoe Airfield.

10 Fireflies from HMS *Indefatigable* would also attack Talanbetoetoe Airfield.

HMS *Indefatigable* would send 2 Fireflies for armed reconnaissance of Mana Airfield.

For Photographic Reconnaissance: 2 Hellcats from HMS *Indomitable*, and ASR 2 Walrus from HMS *Illustrious*.

The weather condition at the planned take off time of 06.15 hours was poor, causing a delay of 25 minutes after which there was a break in the storms allowing the aircraft to start taking off.

125

Strike One Avenger Wing had the same Strike leader as Meridian One, Lt. Col. Stuart RNVR, and consisted of 12 Avengers from 857 Squadron, HMS *Indomitable*, and 12 Avengers from 849 Squadron (Lt. Cdr. Foster), HMS *Victorious*.

The Strike Two Wing consisted of 12 Avengers from 854 Squadron (Lt. Cdr. Mainprice), HMS *Illustrious*, 12 Avengers from 820 Squadron (Lt. Cdr. Luke), HMS *Indefatigable*.

Once Force 63 arrived in the flying off position on Monday, 29th January, there was some concern because of the heavy rain, so the take off was postponed for a time, until there was a break in the weather at 06.40 when the aircraft started taking off, but still the rain came back. The strike force was finally ready to leave at just after 07.30, which was the planned time. The Ramrod Sweeps were quickly away and arrived at their prearranged time over the target, but found little evidence of aircraft on the ground, and it was thought that the Japanese had already got their aircraft in the air.

Although one Avenger ditched soon after take-off, the remaining Avengers, carrying 4 x 500lb bombs, were to be escorted by the rocket firing Fireflies, with Corsairs and Hellcats, which once assembled in the air had set off for their target at the Songei Gerong refinery.

By 09.00hrs the attack by Avengers was ongoing, but what had been improved were the heavy AA defences, which 857 Squadron found out as the first squadron to go in for the attack. Again the barrage balloons were sent up just as the aircraft arrived over the target and the strike leader asked the Fireflies to deal with them. Immediately they were in amongst heavy AA fire which was proving to be very accurate in height and range, but the concentration of fire from the guns on the Fireflies was helpful to the Avengers, who were now engaged in their bombing run.

However, they were still exposed to some enemy fighters, which were diving down on them. Despite the attention paid to the balloons by the Fireflies, few were shot down. Some Avenger pilots stayed above the barrage balloons, but for the Avenger pilots going below balloon height of 4,000ft, there was the need for concentration on avoiding the wires to the balloons. A number of aircraft could not avoid the wires and crashed. One Avenger pilot who crashed due to hitting the wires to a barrage balloon, was Lt. Commander Mainprice RN, Commanding Officer of 854 Squadron on HMS *Illustrious*, who had taken over command of the squadron when it was first commissioned in Squanton, USA. Another Avenger pilot from 854 Squadron who was third in line to the C.O. was also below balloon height and witnessed the CO hitting the cable with his port wing sending his Avenger into a spin and then crashing:

'I thought the C.O. would miss the cable by going around it, but I also saw the next Avenger, also from 854 Squadron, behind the C.O.'s aircraft, hit the same cable. I was shocked and could not believe that the same mistake could be made twice, but made sure that I avoided the cable. I saw my intended target directly below, exactly as it looked on the refinery model on board the carrier.

After dropping my bombs, which completely destroyed the target, I levelled out and flew quite low through the rising smoke cloud from the bombing and headed for the coast while firing at anything we thought worth hitting, and that included AA batteries, vehicles, huts and communication towers.'

Sub. Lt. (A) Frank Stovin-Bradford, of 857 Squadron, was on the way to his target when the observer reported that a Tojo fighter was coming in for an attack on them, causing the air gunner to open fire, but they were still hit quite badly. While the strike force forged ahead, the damaged aircraft still managed to arrive at the target area. Sub. Lt. Stovin-Bradford started his dive through the balloons and dropped his 4 x 500lb bombs on his target while his Avenger received further damaged by AA fire and then left to make his way back to the fleet, but over an extended route to the south-east of Sumatra worked out by his navigator. It was during this time that he realised that the intense training he had received was now paying off. When they came in sight of the fleet, they ditched and all got into their dinghy. The crew were rescued by HMS *Wessex*, which took them back to Australia where they re-joined HMS *Indomitable*. This was the end of Sub. Lt. (A) Frank Stovin-Bradford's combat flying after failing his flying medical, and he then returned home to the UK on a troopship.

Major Hay, Air Coordinator

Major Hay, the Air Coordinator who was flying and observing, started taking photographs at 08.50 just as the bombing started, and from his observations some targets were severely hit, as was confirmed by his photographs. He reported that 'Bombing by No.1 Wing was truly impressive'. No 1 Wing was the Avengers of 857 and 849 squadrons. However, he reported that by the time No 2 Wing started bombing it was getting difficult to see, possibly from the smoke and fires created by the No 1 Wing strike. He commented that 854 Squadron hit the oil tanks and were very close to their set targets, despite losing their Commanding Officer and another of their Avengers to the balloon cables. By the time 820 Squadron started their bombing run they were unable to see their targets, but as Major Hay reported 'quite rightly, chose another'.

Major Hay was not immune from attack and after the last aircraft had bombed, he stopped photographing and climbed from 6,000ft to 10,000 feet in order 'to take vertical line overlap photographs as the flak had died down'. Major Hay:

> 'I soon had to change my mind as a Tojo was coming for us. In shooting this one down, we descended to 0 feet and attracted by the gunfire, an Oscar came along, and by 09.05 he, too, was dead.'

After the strike, the Avengers started making their way to the rendezvous 30 miles away, but some had difficulty in finding it, as did Major Hay who stated, 'Nor could I from 7,000 feet, even though I searched for some time.' Major Hay was busy during the return to base seeing if any enemy aircraft were following, and after the returning aircraft had crossed the coastline:

> 'I examined Lake Ranau for any survivors, but saw none. I then proceeded to the submarine rendezvous for the aircrews forced down and took oblique photographs of all the river mouths in the bay in question.'

May Hay's report on Meridian One and Two concludes:

'Meridian One and Two have been the most interesting and successful operations I know of. In both cases we succeeded in our object and I would like to praise the determination of the Avenger pilots who bombed so accurately in the face of maximum discouragement.

The fighter escort proved itself against the most serious air opposition it has so far met.'

Photographic Reconnaissance taken by Major Hay, and more taken later, revealed that most targets had direct hits and were set on fire, and the losses from combat with the escort fighters claimed 7 destroyed and another 3 possibly destroyed. However, the British losses over the target included four Avengers, one Firefly and one Corsair. Other aircraft were either damaged by enemy fighters or by AA fire and nine aircraft were forced to ditch in the sea, with eight of the nine crews being rescued.

The Fireflies reconnaissance on Mana Airfield was interesting because all they found in terms of activity was a football match!

Meanwhile Task Force 63 had identified an enemy aircraft in their area, and Seafires on CAP intercepted the aircraft, which was a Dinah, and shot it down. Further enemy aircraft were seen in the area, but were chased away by Seafires and Corsairs.

All the strike aircraft had landed by 11.00 hours and approximately 50 minutes later further enemy planes were sighted after been seen on radar, which then attacked the fleet, but with the interception of Seafires they broke away. The enemy formation of one Helen and six Sallies attacked the fleet at a height of about 50 feet. The guns opened up from the ships and it is thought that one aircraft struck was directly attributed to their shooting. Although most of the attacking enemy aircraft managed to get through to the fleet, they broke up from the intended bombing attacks on HMS *Illustrious* and HMS *Indefatigable* when the Seafires intercepted, and most were shot down.

The total loss from both strikes on Pladjoe and Songei Gerong was costly for Task Force 63, with the loss of 41 aircraft. Breaking the total down it was found that 16 aircraft were lost through enemy action, 11 by ditching in the sea and 14 lost through deck crashes. However, the Japanese losses were worse and amounted to 38 aircraft destroyed on the ground, 30 in the air, with a further 7 probably lost in the air.

One of the problems in the Meridian Two attacks was that the Japanese were better prepared and able to deploy aircraft to attack the strike force even before it arrived over the target, and there was increased heavy defensive fire around the target area. Despite this and the heavy cost to the strike force, the raids were successful in stopping production for a number of months and for the oil refineries never to be able to return to the previous production output. This was to put a huge strain on the supply of aviation fuel for the Japanese aircraft.

It was well known that the Japanese had warned that any pilot captured would be executed, and in this action a number of Fleet Air Arm pilots had bailed out and had been captured by the Japanese and taken to Singapore. True to their warning, the Japanese cruelly tortured their prisoners and then executed them. It was thought that nine airmen survived the Palembang raids and were captured by the Japanese. They were then taken to Singapore for further interrogation. However, all evidence of what happened to them was carefully destroyed, but statements obtained from Japanese officers involved in their final hours, appear to confirm that a few days after the broadcast of the Japanese Emperor about their surrender to the Allies, on the 15th August 1945, the nine airmen were beheaded and their bodies disposed of in the sea. The Japanese officers were not going to face trial for their brutal action because they each committed suicide.

Dangers of 'friendly fire'
One of the problems with defensive gunfire from the fleet was that they tended to cause some damage to their own aircraft in the heat of battle by friendly fire. For example, a Supermarine Walrus amphibian had just landed on HMS *Illustrious* after rescuing aircrew from the water, when two Japanese fighters attacked the carrier, flying along its flight deck. However, gunfire from the cruiser HMS *Euryalus* was aimed at the two Japanese aircraft and

instead of stopping firing as the aircraft passed over the HMS *Illustrious* flight deck, they hit the flight deck and the Walrus, which was destroyed, resulting in 12 killed and 21 wounded, including some of the rescued airmen from 'friendly fire'. However, this was not always the case, and when a number of Hellcats were ordered to keep clear because of the ships anti-aircraft firing on aircraft attacking them, one Hellcat pilot did not, and was shot down mistakenly and killed.

Of the Japanese aircraft that managed to reach the British Fleet to attack, which was thought to be seven in total, all were shot down, mainly by the Seafires, Corsairs and Hellcats and it was thought that only one was shot down by the gunfire from the ships. It was often the fighters who had the first opportunity to attack the incoming fighters, but for those enemy aircraft that got through, the CAP fighters often resorted to diving at great risk through the AA fire from their own ships to deal with them.

Later in the day, Task Force 63 set sail and joined up with TF 69 for refuelling on the 30th January, for their voyage to Freemantle, Australia. They arrived in Freemantle on the 4th February and while there an inquiry was held on board HMS *Illustrious* into the 'friendly fire' incident.

The Commander in Chief of the British Pacific Fleet ordered that the fleet to be split into two parts, named 'Able' and 'Baker'. Able Group included HMS *Indomitable*, HMS *Illustrious*, HMS *Indefatigable*, HMS, *Argonaut*, HMS *Black Prince*, HMS *Grenville*, HMS *Undine*, HMS *Undaunted*, HMS *Wager* and HMS *Wessex* which sailed for Sydney later on the 4th February.

Baker Group included HMS *King George V* (Flag Ship of Vice Admiral Sir Henry Bernard Rawlings 2nd in charge British Pacific Fleet), HMS *Victorious*, HMS *Euryalus*, HMS *Kempenfelt*, HMS *Whirlwind*, HMS *Whelp*, HMS *Wakeful*, and HMS *Ursa* which sailed the next day for Sydney.

While at sea, and in line with previous procedure, the fleet carried out practice exercises in gunnery, dive bombing and fleet manoeuvres in emergency situations. It was also important to engage in methods of communication, including radio and radar, especially for the future work with the US Navy.

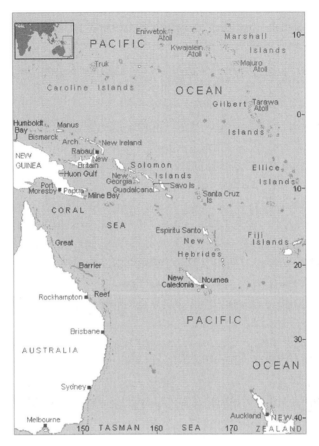

British Pacific Fleet arrival at Sydney, Australia, and the Pacific Ocean area. Courtesy of Gordon Smith www.naval-history.net

When the British Pacific Fleet had arrived in Sydney six days after leaving Freemantle, Admiral Frazer established a base ashore as Commander in Chief, and Vice-Admiral Sir Bernard Rawlings, who was his second in command, was on the battleship HMS *King George V* to command the fleet, with Rear-Admiral Vian as the Flag Officer of the Carrier Squadron, on board HMS *Indomitable*.

When the fleet sailed into Sydney there was a massive welcome from thousands of Australians, despite it being quite early in the morning. After mooring, Admiral Sir Bruce Fraser, Commander in

Chief of the British Pacific Fleet, welcomed on board HMS *King George V*, Admiral Sir Guy Royle, Commonwealth Naval Board, and Rear Admiral G.D. Moore, Flag Officer in Charge, Sydney, who were introduced to the Commanding Officers of the British Pacific Fleet.

HMS Indomitable arrival at Sydney.   *Geoffrey Wright Collection*

Docking in Sydney.   *Geoffrey Wright Collection*

The Australians were very pleased to see the British Fleet and showed great hospitality to the British sailors who had been given 48 hours shore leave. The Fleet remained at Sydney to undertake repairs and the Australians also assisted the Fleet with very good facilities for refit and repairs right through until the end of the war.

HMS Indomitable entering Captain Cook Dry Dock   . Geoffrey Wright Collection

Sydney Harbour, Garden Island Naval Base.   Courtesy of Paul Whiteing

134

The facilities included the Captain Cook Graving Dock at Garden City Island, Sydney, which was used for the emergency docking of HMS *Illustrious* even before it was officially opened. Further additions to the British Pacific Fleet were added, with ships from the Australian Navy and New Zealand Navy. A land base had already been established and commissioned as HMS Golden Hind, as a barracks and administrative centre for the British Pacific Fleet in the Woolloomooloo Bay area.

MONABs (Mobile Naval Operating Air Bases)

MONABs were self-contained, mobile units formed to take over airfields and convert them into fully operational airfields for maintenance and repair of aircraft from the British Pacific Fleet. MONAB 1 was the first units set up at Nowra NSW in 1945.

In 1941 a new civilian aerodrome was opened at Nowra, NSW, with work being undertaken on an accommodation camp for RAAF Personnel. By 1942, RAAF Nowra was in operation for Torpedo Bombing training. The station was also used by the USAAC (United States Army Air Corps) and the Netherlands East Indies Air Force B-26 bombers, from 1942-1944, for practice on the bombing and torpedo ranges. The practice for torpedo bombing was on target ships in Jervis Bay.

In 1944 Nowra was selected by the Admiralty as a station that was suitable for maintaining and servicing carrier based aircraft while the carriers of the British Pacific Fleet were docked in Sydney. Nowra officially became a Royal Naval Air Station (RNAS) on January 2nd 1945, being commissioned as HMS Nabbington and the base for MONAB 1. The development of the airfield continued throughout January, with the first 6 Corsairs from 1833 Squadron on HMS *Illustrious* arriving at RNAS Nowra on the 9th February.

The next day, the 10th February, aircraft from three other carriers arrived from Sydney. These were 820 Squadron Avengers from HMS *Indefatigable*, along with 849 Squadron's Avengers, and 1834 and 1836 Squadron's Corsairs from HMS *Victorious*, 857 Squadron Avengers, and 1839 and 1844 Squadron's Hellcats from HMS *Indomitable*. The final arrival was 854 Squadron Avengers from HMS *Illustrious* on the 11th February. This was to be the start of regular transfer of aircraft from the carriers docked in Sydney for maintenance and repair.

There were a total of 10 MONABs, and as well as MONAB 1 at RNAS Nowra there were two other MONABS in the Sydney area. MONAB 2 was at RNAS Bankstown, commissioned on the 29th January 1945, and MONAB 3 was RNAS Schofields, commissioned on the 18th February 1945. MONAB 2 and 3 was in the suburbs of Sydney, and other MONABS in Australia were MONAB 5 at RNAS Jervis Bay, south of Sydney and near to RNAS Nowra. MONAB 6 RNAS at Maryborough, 160 miles north of Brisbane, and MONAB 7 RNAS Archerfield in the Brisbane area. Also in Brisbane was TAMY 1 (Transportable Aircraft Maintenance Yard No 1) at Rocklea Camp RNAS Nabsford,

Further MONABS were MONAB 4 at RNAS Ponam in the Admiralty Islands, and MONAB 8 at RNAS Lai-Tak (Hong Kong) from the 26th September, 1945, and MONAB 9 RNAS Sembewang (Singapore) from the 5th October, both after the surrender of the Japanese. MONAB 10 (HMS Nabhurst) was not formed until August 1945, at the time of the Japanese surrender and did not leave the UK.

CHAPTER 15

The Fleet Train

The US Navy was used to working in the huge expanse of the Pacific Ocean and had a well organised system of re-supply, which was their 'Fleet Train', consisting of tankers for refuelling, supply ships, including refrigerated ships and ammunition ships. This system would allow the ships to remain at sea for long periods and continue operations without having to rely on re-supply at land bases.

It was a different experience for the British ships which had been designed to operate and defend the British Isles, and thus could re-supply at land bases, but were not used to operations in the huge expanse of the Pacific Ocean. The British Pacific Fleet would need to be able to support itself far away from their land bases, and the British version of the 'Fleet Train' of approximately 60 ships was assembled, consisting of Royal Navy ships, Royal Fleet Auxiliary and supply ships from other British allies. The Fleet Train was to be under the command of Rear Admiral D. B. Fisher.

The British Pacific Fleet had been allocated Manus Island in the Admiralty Islands as its intermediate base and on the 24 February the fleet sailed for its base at Manus. While at sea no time was lost in training, and practice was undertaken in air gunnery and also replenishment while at sea. It was important that the fleet also practiced US Navy procedures in fleet formations and manoeuvres, including communication arrangements.

By this time the USN Navy had a well organised system after many years in the Pacific, whereas the British Pacific Fleet was largely untried and a system of working together as a team was necessary. The problem of refuelling at sea by British tankers was the trailing hoses over the stern of the tankers, while the Americans had perfected a speeder system of ships refuelling alongside the tanker. The time taken over refuelling the British ships was a serious problem, increasing the possibility of attack by enemy submarines.

British Oiler of the Fleet Train.   Courtesy of Paul Whiteing

Development of refuelling alongside a tanker. Courtesy of Paul Whiteing

Another problem was the lack of refrigerated space compared to the American ships, which increased the number of times ships

138

had to be replenished while at sea. However, despite the concern of some in the American Navy, it was the final decision by Admiral Nimitz that the British Pacific Fleet would be best used in the Operation Iceberg series to cover the invasion of Okinawa.

The British Pacific Fleet was allocated Task Force Numbers linked to the US Navy procedures, and Task Force 113, consisting of the 1st Battle Squadron, 1st Aircraft Carriers Squadron, 4th Cruiser Squadron and 25th, 4th and 27th Destroyer Flotillas and the Fleet Train, became 'Task Force 112'. Task Force 113 was eventually designated 'Task Force 57'.

The British Pacific Fleet 'Fleet Train' Task Force 112

The ships in the Fleet Train were under the command of Rear Admiral Fisher in HMS *Tyne* (Destroyer Depot Ship), and included ships for replenishment of armaments, repairs, distilling, Naval stores, Air maintenance and repairs, Landing Ships, Water Carriers, Victualling, Fleet Oilers, Fleet Accommodation, Store Ships, Hospital Ships, Tugs and Net Layers. There were the escort carriers for replenishment of aircraft and aircrews, and escort carriers used for ferrying aircraft duties across the oceans, a Command ship Logistical Supply Group and destroyers and escort vessels for protection duties of the Fleet Train.

Task Force 113 Sails from Sydney, Australia

The 1st Aircraft Carrier Squadron that included HMS *Indomitable* (Flag of Rear Admiral Sir Philip Vian), HMS *Victorious* and HMS *Indefatigable*, under the protection of the destroyers HMAS *Quickmatch* (D4), HMAS *Quiberon*, HMS *Queenborough* and HMS *Quality*, sailed from Sydney on the 27th February 1945, to carry out exercises and fly on aircraft before joining the rest of the British Pacific Fleet on the 28th February. HMS *Illustrious* was due to sail with the other carriers, but had problems with her propeller and needed repairs, joining the fleet later.

The Fleet aircraft were to fly from RNAS Nowra to join the carriers on the 27th February, including 820 Squadron Avengers to HMS *Indefatigable*, 849 Squadron Avengers, 1834 and 1836

139

Squadron Corsairs to HMS *Victorious,* and 1839 and 1844 Squadron Hellcats to HMS *Indomitable*. On the 28th February, 857 Squadron Avengers flew to HMS *Indomitable*. The final flights were to HMS *Illustrious*, when on the 6th March, 854 Squadron Avengers flew to the carrier, followed on the 7th March by 1830 and 1833 Squadron Corsairs.

The next day, sailings included the battleships HMS *King George V* (Flag Vice Admiral Sir Henry Bernard Rawlings 1st Battle Squadron and 2nd in Charge British Pacific Fleet) and HMS *Howe,* maintenance carrier HMS *Unicorn*, with light cruisers HMS *Swiftsure* (Flag Rear Admiral E.J.P. Brind), HMS *Argonaut*, HMS *Black Prince*, HMS *Euryalus* (Flag ship Rear Admiral J.H. Edelsten) and HMNZS *Gambia*, destroyers HMS *Grenville*, HMS *Ulster*, HMS *Undine*, HMS *Ursa* and HMS *Urania,* HMS *Kempenfelt*, HMS *Wager*, HMS *Wakeful*, HMS *Whirlwind*, HMS *Whelp* and HMS *Wessex*. The weather after leaving Sydney was rough with gales and it was in the afternoon that both the 1st Carrier Squadron and Task Force 113 rendezvoused. TF 113 then changed course to the north until and further refuelling of ships that needed topping up, was also conducted successfully.

Although it was still rough weather, the Task Force had to be constantly at the ready for enemy attacks and carried out various practice exercises and manoeuvres during the day, although the plans to operate night fighters from HMS *Indomitable* was held up because of poor weather conditions. However, on the 7th March when TF 113 was nearing Manus, further training exercises were carried out when land based Corsairs from the island carried out simulated torpedo, strafing and kamikaze 'suicide' attacks with a CAP (Combat Air Support) provided by Hellcats and Seafires protecting the fleet. These exercises provided an important experience for the fleet in advance of their future combat operations.

After completing the practice exercises, TF113 entered Manus harbour and anchored. During the period the ships were anchored refuelling was carried out, but the experience of the heavy swells that occurred in the Pacific anchorages were a concern to the British Pacific Fleet and the example of the US Navy steel catamarans were proven to be more effective than those used by the British. The US Navy was very helpful to the British Fleet and provided steel catamarans until the British were in a position to provide their own.

CHAPTER 16

The Allied Submarines in the Pacific War

The work of the Allied submarines in the Pacific War was important, not just for sinking the Japanese and German vessels in the Indian and Pacific Oceans, but was a lifeline for aircrew, through their lifeguard duties, rescuing airmen that bailed out from a crashing aircraft, run out of fuel or had ditched in the sea. Many aviators owe their lives to the work of the Allied submarines, as well as the flying boats that undertook SAR (Search and Rescue) duties, and their story is told below.

The American Submarines

On 7th December 1941, the Japanese attacked and sank many of the US Pacific Fleet ships in Pearl Harbour. However, they missed the submarine base and were to regret that when the American submarines were ordered by Admiral R Stark, Chief of Naval Operations in Washington, apparently without the US government approval, to 'execute unrestricted submarine warfare on Japan'. This Japanese attack on Pearl Harbour brought America into the war.

The American submarines were tasked on various types of missions, including hunting and sinking Japanese shipping, reconnaissance, landing special forces and SAR (Search and Rescue), saving the many pilots who had ditched in the sea. The American submarines were fast, long range, and had air conditioning, which made them comfortable to work and live in, especially in the tropics. However, there were problems in the early days with faulty torpedoes, but once this had been corrected, their success in sinking enemy ships was greatly enhanced.

SAR (Search and Rescue)

One of the special missions carried out in the Pacific War by the US submarines, which were appreciated by aviators, was in the rescue of airmen that ditched in the sea. Once the strike aircraft had taken off from their carriers to attack their targets, they knew that if they were hit or ran out of fuel, they would have to bail out over land or ditch in the sea. Their hope of survival was not very good if they came down on land, because if captured by the Japanese it was well known that aircrew would certainly be tortured for information and then executed. Pilots were aware that for each mission there would be submarines stationed off the islands they were attacking, for a few days to rescue any aircrew that made their way to the coast. Should they ditch in the sea, the same submarines would be on the lookout for them, and often be guided to the airmen by the American Dumbo aircraft. The British aircraft carrier also had two Walrus amphibian aircraft, known as 'Darby and Joan', which took part in SAR, rescuing many pilots that had ditched in the sea.

Freemantle Submarine Base

The United States submarines arrived in Freemantle in 1942, where a new submarine repair facility was built. The Fremantle Submarine Base became the second largest Allied submarine base in the Pacific after Pearl Harbour, in World War II.

Later in 1944 the Eighth Flotilla, consisting of British and Dutch submarines, was transferred to Fremantle and based there during the Pacific War. From there they would sail out and operate in the Java Sea, while under the command of the US 7th Fleet.

It was important and necessary to have such a presence in Australia, because Japanese submarines were patrolling off the Western Australian coast. However, many Australians knew very little about having such an important submarine base on their shores, because of the secrecy of the operations that were operating out of the base.

Other ships were also using Freemantle, including merchant ships, battleships, hospital ships and troopships that were pre-war ocean liners and had been requisitioned for war service, including the RMS *Queen Mary* and RMS *Queen Elizabeth*.

143

British Submarines

Submarines from the British Eastern Fleet were sailing out of their base in Trincomalee, Ceylon, and patrolling the Bay of Bengal, Straits of Malacca, up to Singapore and along the western coast of Sumatra, in the Indian Ocean from 1943, and were responsible for sinking Japanese cargo vessels supplying their occupation forces in Burma. The success of the British submarines by March 1945 was in gaining control of the Malacca Straits which completely cut off supplies by sea from reaching the Japanese in Burma.

On the 11th January 1944, two British submarines had success when HMS *Tally Ho* sighted the light cruiser *Kuma*, which was on anti-submarine patrol out of Penang, and sank her with two torpedo strikes. Later in January, the light cruiser *Kitakami* was on convoy duty and while in the Malacca Straits was hit and damaged by two torpedoes from HMS *Templer*. The *Kitakami* was towed and repaired in Seletar Naval Base, Singapore. This was followed on the 17th July 1944, by HMS *Telemachus,* while patrolling in the Malacca Straits, seeking out and sinking the Japanese submarine *1-166,* with the loss of 88 and10 survivors.

The British submarines were also seeking out and attacking German U-boats operating out of Penang, a base they shared with the Imperial Japanese Navy. The British Submarine HMS *Trenchant* while on patrol near Penang in the Malacca Straits, sank the German U-boat *U-859* on the 23rd September 1944, with a loss of 47 and 20 survivors.

On the 8th June 1945, the Japanese heavy cruiser *Ashigara* was sailing in the Banka Strait, off south east Sumatra, while carrying 1,600 troops from Java to Singapore, and escorted by the destroyer *Kamikazi*. The three Allied submarines, USS *Blueback*, HMS *Trenchant* and HMS *Stygian* were on patrol, and when they spotted the two Japanese ships they attacked. The Japanese destroyer *Kamakazi* fired on HMS *Trenchant*, which submerged and then fired eight torpedoes at *Ashigari*, causing her to capsize. Only 400 of the 1,600 troops on board were saved, along with 853 of the crew by the *Kamikaze*.

After the Eighth Flotilla of the British and Dutch submarines had transferred to Freemantle, the Fourth Flotilla and the newly formed Second Flotilla remained in Trincomalee. When the Eighth Flotilla transferred to Subic Bay in the Philippines, the Fourth Flotilla took over in Freemantle.

Overall, the British and Dutch submarines successfully sank seven Japanese warships, as well as a significant number of merchant ships, but the main focus of the submarines was tracking and dealing with coastal trade off Malaysia and in the South China and Java seas.

The British X-craft (midget submarines) were first designed to attack the German battleship *Tirpitz* which was anchored in a Norwegian fjord where it was difficult to attack by other means. On the 22nd September 1943, six X-craft went on the mission, and two managed to get through the defences and successfully put the *Tirpitz* out of action for the rest of the war.

The X-craft were used in the Pacific War and included sinking a Japanese cruiser, when on the 31st July 1945, XE-1 and XE-3 attacked and sank the Japanese heavy cruiser *Takao* off Singapore.

During service in the Pacific, three British submarines were lost. HMS *Stonehenge* was lost in unknown circumstances while patrolling out of Trincomalee, between the Sumatra and Nicobar Islands in March 1944. In November 1944, HMS *Stratagem* was sunk by a Japanese destroyer, and in January 1945, HMS *Porpoise* was mine laying off Penang when it is thought to have been sunk by Japanese aircraft.

By the middle of 1945, the Imperial Japanese Navy had received constant attention from the Allies' submarines and had become a much weakened force. Furthermore, many of the merchant ships that had been attacked and sunk by the Allies had left the Japanese a much reduced cargo carrying capacity, thus forcing them to resort to using their submarines for resupply. Due to the areas of the Pacific that had been invaded and occupied by the Japanese forces, the only way their troops could effectively be supplied was by sea, and the lack of protection of their own merchant shipping became their downfall.

Part 4: Sakishima Gunto: The 'unsinkable aircraft carriers'

CHAPTER 17

Operation Iceberg One

The main objective for 'Operation Iceberg' was for the American amphibious forces to capture Okinawa and then use it as a base for attacking the main islands of Japan. It was to be the objective of the British Pacific Fleet to attack the airfields in the Sakishima Gunto (Islands) to prevent the Japanese using them as staging posts between Formosa (Taiwan) and Okinawa for kamikaze aircraft and other aircraft for maintaining and supplying their forces on Okinawa. The Sakishima Gunto consists of three main larger islands, Miyako, Ishigaki and Iriomote, with number of smaller islands.

Prior to the arrival of the British Pacific Fleet, the US Navy Task Force 58, consisting of 10 large carriers, 6 smaller carriers supported by battleships, cruisers and destroyers, had been anchored in Ulithi for R&R and replenishment, refuelling and rearming, before sailing on the 14th March to prepare for the Okinawa campaign. Their first task was to target the airfields bases on Kyushi, where Japan could launch air strikes on the Okinawa invasion, the naval bases at Kobe and Kure, and the Ryukyu Islands. The Ryukyu Islands, also known as the 'Ryukyu Arc', are a chain of volcanic islands that stretch from Kyushu to Formosa (Taiwan), and are known by the Japanese as the 'Nansei' Islands.

After refuelling and taking on provisions, the British Pacific Fleet continued with exercise training at sea. This was until the 15th March when Admiral Rawlings received orders from Admiral Nimitz for Task Force 113 and Task Force 112 to report for duty in Operation Iceberg, supporting the Okinawa landings.

From receiving the orders, all exercises were cancelled and the fleet undertook topping up of the fuel that had been used during exercises, loading ammunition, and making sure stores and aircraft and crews that had been training ashore had been embarked in advance of the first vessels sailing from Manus on the 17th March.

The Fleet Train oiling force, designated 'TU 112.2.1', consisting of RFA *Cedardale*, MV *San Ambrosio* and *San Adolpho*, with the escort carrier HMS *Striker* carrying replacement aircraft, and escorted by destroyer HMS *Whirlwind,* Frigate HMS *Findhorn* and Sloop HMS *Crane,* sailed from Manus to ensure that they would be in position to refuel the British Pacific Fleet when they arrived in their operational area off the Sakishima Gunto. At the same time, another Fleet Train force designated 'TU 112.2.5' with escort carrier HMS *Speaker* with Squadron 1840 Hellcats onboard for CAP duties for the fleet train, was escorted by the destroyer HMS *Kempenfelt* and Sloop HMS *Pheasant*.

Task Force 113 sailed for Manus on the 18th March at 06.00 hours and comprised of HMS *King George V*, HMS *Howe*, HMS *Swiftsure*, HMS *Argonaut*, HMNZS *Gambia*, protected by the destroyers HMS *Grenville*, HMS *Ulster*, HMS *Undine*, HMS *Urania* and HMS *Undaunted*. However, the aircraft carriers HMS *Illustrious*, HMS *Indefatigable*, HMS *Indomitable* and HMS *Victorious* had been delayed due to embarkation of aircraft and adverse weather conditions, but sailed later at 11.00am under the protection of destroyers for the American main advance base at Ulithi Atoll, for refuelling before sailing for the Sakishima Islands.

While working in the tropics the heat was intense, especially for the sailors on board the British vessels, and it was well known that you could fry an egg on the steel deck of an aircraft carrier. The Royal Navy ships were originally designed and built mainly to operate in the more temperate climates and lacked air-conditioning and provision for making enough fresh water for drinking and water for washing and showering by the crew. When in the intense heat of the Pacific areas, sailors were not only under the stress of active service in combat zones, but also became stressed when water supplies were rationed. Furthermore, keeping the fleet supplied while in the Pacific Ocean was a huge problem, but some of these problems were helped by the US Navy bases which assisted in refuelling and other essential supplies for aircraft repairs.

While on course for Ulithi Atoll in the Caroline Islands, Task Force 113 continued with practice manoeuvres for the forthcoming combat and protection of ships from enemy aircraft, and on the 20th March the first ships of the fleet reached Ulithi Atoll and entered the harbour. In the afternoon the aircraft carriers arrived, and the first task was to refuel and take on ammunition. This took place over several days.

While the British Pacific Fleet was anchored at Ulithi Atoll, Vice Admiral C.H. McMorris, U.S.N, and Captain H.S. Hopkins, R.N., British Pacific Fleet Liaison Officer, arrived by seaplane from Guam on the 22nd March for discussions with Vice Admiral Rawlings. Although Admiral Nimitz had intended to come as well, he had to decline because he was not well. It was an opportunity to invite the Flag Officers of the British Pacific Fleet to lunch on board HMS *King George V* for them to meet Vice Admiral McMorris.

The British Pacific Fleet sailed from Ulithi Atoll at 07.15 hours on the 23rd March under its new designation of 'Task Force 57', first to the refuelling area on the 25th March, which was not without difficulty due to strong winds and choppy sea, combined with problems with the hoses from the tankers. During the refuelling period, CAP (Combat Air Patrol) duties were provided by aircraft from HMS *Speaker*.

After this was completed, Task Force 57 proceeded to their operational position for Operation Iceberg, arriving on the 26th March. While en route, Task Force 57 carried out bombardment practice exercises, while aircraft from the carriers with cover maintained CAP (Combat Air Patrols) and ASPS (Anti-Submarine Patrols) during daylight hours.

Task Force 57 consisted of the 1st Battle Squadron TU 57.1 (Task Unit 1), 1st Aircraft Carrier Squadron TU 57.2, 4th Cruiser

Squadron TU 57.4, and Destroyers TU 57.8, including 25th Destroyer Flotilla, 4th Destroyer Flotilla and 27th Destroyer Flotilla.

The Task Units had the following ships:

TU 57.1 1st Battle Squadron:

HMS *King George V* (Flag of Vice Admiral Sir Bernard Rawlings Commander of TF 57) and HMS *Howe*.

TU 57.2 1st Aircraft Carrier Squadron:

HMS *Indomitable* (Flag of Vice Admiral Sir Philip Vain, Second-in-Command TF 57), aircraft: 29 Hellcats and 15 Avengers

HMS *Victorious,* aircraft: 37 Corsairs, 14 Avengers and 2 Walrus amphibians

HMS *Illustrious,* aircraft: 36 Corsairs and 16 Avengers

HMS *Indefatigable,* aircraft: 40 Seafires, 21 Avengers and 12 Fireflies

TU 57.4 4th Cruiser Squadron:

HMS *Swiftsure*, *Black Prince*, *Euryalus*, *Argonaut* and HMNZS *Gambia*

TU 57.8 Destroyers:

25th Destroyer Flotilla: HMS *Grenville*, *Ulster*, *Undine*, *Urania* and *Undaunted*

4th Destroyer Flotilla: HMS *Quickmatch, Quiberon, Queenborough* and *Quality*

27th Destroyer Flotilla: HMS *Whelp* and *Wager*

The British Pacific Fleet Task Force 57 was now under the overall command of Admiral Raymond Spraunce USN, Commander in Chief of the US Fifth Fleet. Task Force 57's job was to prevent the Japanese using the Sakishima Islands in the Ryukyu Island group as stop off points for aircraft, including kamikaze suicide aircraft flying from bases on Formosa (now Taiwan) to attack the surface ships at Okinawa. The Japanese saw these islands as their 'unsinkable aircraft carriers' which, due to the loss of many of their aircraft carriers, was very true. Okinawa was the main island in the Ryukyu group and was half way between Formosa and Kyushu, the most southern of the four major islands of Japan. The Japanese were preparing to defend the Japanese homeland from invasion and Okinawa was needed as a major base to defend Japan.

US Action in the Ryukyu Islands

The Japanese military were not very concerned about the strategic position of the Ryukyu Islands before 1944, and had very few Japanese soldiers stationed on the islands. That is, until America was gathering strength in preparation for the invasion of Japan. They then became aware that the islands would make ideal bases for the long-range American B-27 bombers to attack the Japanese homeland, and commenced the build up of Japanese army, navy and air force personnel on the islands of Miyako and Ishigaki.

American reconnaissance aircraft started collecting photographs of the islands, especially Okinawa, in preparation for its invasion by US amphibious forces, and there were initial strikes on the islands of Miyako and Ishigaki islands in October 1944, and in early 1945. Further bombing attacks took place on the Ryukyu Islands and Okinawa, as part of a 'softening up' for the invasion D-Day, 1st April 1945.

Further strikes were undertaken against the Japanese airfields on the southernmost island of Kyushu by Task Force 58, including aircraft consisting of Hellcats, Helldivers, Corsairs and Avengers from TG 58.1, USS *Hornet CV-12*, USS *Wasp CV-18* and USS *Bennington CV-20*, and light carrier USS *Belleau Wood CVL-24*, and from TG 58.2, USS *Franklin CV-13*, USS *Hancock CV-19* and light carrier USS *San Jacinto CVL-30*, starting on the 18th March. This was followed the next day with fighter sweeps over Honshu and strikes on military installations and airfields. Bomber strikes were focused on the Japanese ships in Kobe harbour.

However, on both days the US ships had been heavily attacked by Japanese fighters and bombers, and it was on the 19th March that USS *Franklin* was hit by two 550lb bombs. The carrier was seriously damaged, with a loss of 724 and 265 wounded. USS *Franklin* was taken in tow on the 20th March and after first calling at Ulithi, sailed to Pearl Harbour, where the carrier received temporary repairs before sailing to the Brooklyn Navy Yard, USA. By the time USS *Franklin* had being fully repaired, it was too late to return to the Pacific because the war had ended.

On the 23rd March 1945, the same day as the British Pacific Fleet Task Force 57 sailed from Ulithi Atoll, aircraft strikes were launched from USS *Hancock* on Miyako airfield, as well as the Okinawa airfields, and continued the next day with strikes on Hirara airfield, docks and ships at Miyako, followed by strikes on Ishigaki airfield and the shipping in the area. This was a warming up to the islands for the forthcoming attacks by the British Pacific Fleet Task Force 57, that had arrived in position for its first strikes on Ishigaki and Miyako. USS *Hancock* then concentrated on further strikes on the Okinawa airfields and ground defences, followed by strikes on a seaplane base and docks in Kagoshima Bay, Kyushu. For the next few days the carrier aircraft would concentrate on further softening up of the defences and airfields, before and after the start of the Okinawa invasion on the 1st April 1945.

Task Force 57 attacks on Ishigaki and Miyako airfields 26 March, 1945

On the 26th March the British Pacific Fleet was positioned approximately 100 miles off the Sakishima islands and ready to attack the airfields and seaplane base with their aircraft that included Hellcats, Corsairs, Seafires, Fireflies and Avengers from the carriers. The Seafires' performance was very good at high altitude and it was decided to use them mainly for CAP (Combat Air Patrol) duties, especially for protection of the fleet from kamikaze suicide attacks.

After the CAP (Combat Air Patrol) aircraft and ASP (Anti-Submarine Patrol) had taken off on the 26th March, the first group of attack aircraft took off at 06.30 hours, with the aircraft attacking the airfields, creating much damage to the runways and destroying Japanese aircraft on the ground.

This was to be the main task for the British Pacific Fleet, keeping the airfields out of action by making it difficult for the Japanese to use the islands as 'stepping stones' for kamikaze aircraft from Formosa to Okinawa to stop off, refuel, and for their pilots to have updated briefings before flying on to their targets. There would also be new aircraft transferring from the factories in Japan, or reinforcement aircraft flying to Okinawa, and some on to Formosa. Most of the aircraft from Formosa were flown by experienced pilots, whereas the aircraft flown from the Japanese homeland would be mainly inexperienced pilots having just been given limited flight training, but seen as suitable pilots for kamikaze suicide attacks.

The British Fighter patrols over the islands of Ishigaki and Miyako reported that after the attacks on the airfields there appeared to be very little activity in the area and they were surprised by the small amount of flak, but this changed as the day wore on, with the flak becoming much heavier. During the afternoon, two Avenger squadrons took part in strikes and had close, middle and top cover, but one Avenger and its crew of 3 from 854 Squadron was lost, along with the Corsair flown by the CO of 1836 Squadron, Lt. Cdr. Tomkinson.

There were air raid warnings given for possible Japanese aircraft attacks on the fleet, and just one Japanese reconnaissance aircraft, a Dinah was seen and chased off, but by then it was known that the position of the fleet would have been reported. Once all aircraft had landed, the fleet sailed out of the area. One Corsair pilot had ditched in the sea and was rescued by a Walrus amphibian. During the hours of darkness the fleet maintained close observation by radar, and aircraft were dispatched to deal with any threats by enemy aircraft.

The next day, further Ramrods were made against Ishigaki, and bomber strikes by two Avenger squadrons were conducted on areas around the airfields, attacking buildings that had not been dealt with in the previous attack. As well as ASR (Air Sea Rescue) from the Walrus amphibian ships, submarines were used to rescue air crew that had ditched in the water. That day HMS *Undine* rescued the Avenger strike leader, who was the Commanding

Officer of 857 Squadron, and his crew, and also found a US Corsair pilot who had been adrift for two days. The same day the American rescue submarine USS *Kingfish* was tasked to rescue American aircrew that had ditched, and was also instructed as rescue submarine for the pilot of a British Avenger from 854 Squadron, who had bailed out after being hit by flak. Sadly, his observer and air gunner was lost. Other losses was one Corsair from 1836 Squadron, which was shot down and the pilot killed, and two Seafires which were lost in deck accidents, also killing the pilots.

Although the Seafires were very successful in the CAP role, landing on deck was not easy for the pilots and often the aircraft would tip forward after landing with the propellers striking the deck. Intense work was being done by the Supermarine team to rectify the problem, and combined with their work and the increased experience of the pilots flying the Seafire, the problem was eventually resolved.

[Details of the work of the Supermarine Team can be found in Chapter 16 of *Spitfire's Forgotten Designer: The Career of Joe Smith*. Mike Roussel, The History Press 2013]

Seafire tips on its nose on landing.   *Frank Stockwell Collection*

The cost to Task Force 57 was 3 Corsairs and 3 Avengers lost in combat and 2 Seafires lost in deck accidents. The cost to aircrew was 9, that included 2 Corsair pilots, 1 Avenger pilot, 2 observers, 2 air gunners and 2 Seafire pilots, all lost.

It had been the aim to continue the strikes against the airfields, but a warning of a possible typhoon reaching the replenishment area, disrupted the refuelling, which led to the fleet withdrawing to refuel and replenishment from the 28th to 30th March in the area named 'Midge'. The replenishment areas for Operation Iceberg were called Mosquito, Midge and Cootie, and were positioned in the Pacific to the west of Luzon in the Philippines. Task Units 112.2.1 and 112.2.5 were in position and the fleet split into two groups. The refuelling group went to Task Unit 112.2.1 while the other group, still in sight, were transferring aircraft. Task Unit 112.2.5 with HMS *Speaker*, HMS *Pheasant* and HMS *Kempenfelt* were to maintain CAP and ASPS.

Attacks to the British Pacific Fleet Task Force 57

The British Pacific Fleet returned to the flying off positions on 31st March and started with ramrod attacks and two Avenger strikes, with one Avenger from 849 Squadron shot down with the loss of its three crew, and another Avenger from 857 Squadron ditching in the sea while the rescue submarine USS *Kingfish* was still on hand to rescue the crew. The 1st April was Easter Sunday, and also 'Okinawa D-day', the start of the initial landings of American amphibious forces on Okinawa. Over 20 aircraft from the Japanese 1st Air Fleet, Formosa, attacked, and a number of the aircraft got through to attack Task Force 57, including their Zeke fighters with one being shot down by a Corsair. The Seafires were on CAP and immediately got into air combat with the enemy, and despite the danger of being hit by friendly fire from their own anti-aircraft guns, still continued attacks on the enemy aircraft.

The US Fifth Fleet, under the command of Admiral Spruance, started their attacks on Okinawa right at the beginning of April, with the US Tenth Army, including US Marines, attacking and landing in the west of the island. The attacks started at first without much opposition from the Japanese, but by the middle of

154

the month there was fierce fighting, which continued through April to June.

The Japanese were aggressive in their defence of Okinawa and intended to hold out as long as possible. Recognising that their navy could no longer successfully challenge the Allied ships, the Japanese resorted to using their pilots to undertake suicide attacks by flying their aircraft into the allied vessels. The kamikaze (Divine Wind) attacks was promoted by Vice-Admiral Takijiro Ohnishi, who wanted a special attack force of aircraft that would dive on the carrier flight decks causing as much damage as possible with the aim of putting the carriers out of action. The Zero fighters used, would also carry a 550lb (250 kg) bomb, but the Japanese pilots saw that taking part in these suicide missions would mean that they would die with honour for their Emperor and nation. These kamikaze attacks were very fierce and there were many losses to ships at sea and to the aircraft.

A6M5 Type 0 model 52 Zero (Zeke).   Bill Pippin Collection

Although the British Pacific Fleet was stationed off the Sakishima islands, they were not immune from the kamikaze attacks, but there was a difference in the build of the American carriers and the British carriers. The American carriers had wooden flight decks and any kamikaze aircraft striking the deck would go through the decks and into the hangers, causing massive damage and killing and injuring many sailors. As well as the fires resulting from strike, many carriers were sunk or severely damaged causing

155

them to go into US dockyards for up to six months for repairs. The British carriers on the other hand had steel armoured flight decks, and although damage to the carriers was suffered, it was not as serious as that of the American carriers.

It was early in the morning on the 1st April when Hellcat fighters took off from the British carriers to maintain a presence over Ishigaki and Miyako, but not long after, Japanese aircraft were detected by radar and Hellcats were sent to intercept the enemy, while Corsairs and Seafires took off to also meet the incoming aircraft. In the ensuing battle the Corsairs shot down one aircraft, the Seafires, two aircraft, and the Hellcats that had been recalled, dispatched one aircraft. Just after 07.00 hours the Japanese aircraft attacked the fleet, which had been alerted and were ready to put up a heavy defence. One Zeke was chased by Seafires from 887 Squadron, but dived on HMS *Indefatigable* hitting the flight deck and the base of the island, creating a large hole. It took out the briefing room when its 500lb bomb exploded, causing serious damage to the sick bay and briefing room. As a result of this attack, 4 officers and 10 ratings were killed and 16 wounded. HMS *Indomitable* was also attacked by an Oscar flying at low level and strafing with its machine gun, spraying the flight deck, with the casualties from that attack resulting in 1 killed and 6 wounded. The same aircraft then flew on, to machine gun HMS *King George V* without causing any casualties. Due to the armoured decks of the British carriers, the fires were quickly put out and the flight deck of the carrier was cleared within one hour.

The first bombing strikes on Ishigaki airfield and its runways revealed little evidence of aircraft on the ground, but later in the afternoon the air patrols identified enemy aircraft on Ishigaki and Hirari airfields, and these were attacked by fighters, destroying 14 aircraft and damaging other aircraft on the ground. One enemy aircraft dived on HMS *Victorious*, but she was already swinging away and the wing of the aircraft hit the deck and plunged into the sea with its bomb exploding harmlessly in the water. The destroyer HMS *Ulster* was also damaged by a Japanese bomb causing her to lose power, but remained afloat. She was towed to Leyte by HMNZ *Gambia* for temporary repairs before returning to the UK. One Seafire crashed when landing on HMS *Victorious*, killing the pilot.

Attacks on the airfields on Ishigaki and Miyako of the Sakishima Gunto continued with the runways being put out of action, but the Japanese still managed to fill in the cratered runways during the hours of darkness. This was a continuing theme, with daytime raids cratering the runways, and night time repairs made easier because they were built of crushed coral, for which there were plentiful supplies locally. Just before Task Force 57 withdrew on the afternoon of the 2nd April for refuelling in Area Midge, four kamikazes attacked, but were avoided by the ships. While out of the area US Task Group 58.1 carriers kept up the pressure on the islands.

Task Group 58.1 strike the Sakishima Gunto

USS *Hornet*: CV-12 Air Group 2, F6F Hellcats (VB-17), TBM Avengers (VT-17), SB2C Helldivers (VB-17)

USS *Bennington*: CV-20 Air Group 82 F6F Hellcats VF 82, SB2C Helldivers VB-82 F4U Corsairs VMF-123

USS *Belleau Wood*: CVL-24 Air Group 30 F6F Hellcats VF30 TBM Avengers VT30

On the 3rd April, USS *Hornet* CV-12, USS *Bennington* CV-20 and USS *Belleau Wood* CVL-24 launched continuous strikes on the airfield runways, installations and shipping around the islands of Miyako and Ishigaki. Miyako had three airfields, the Japanese Navy Hirara airfield, the Japanese Army Norbara airfield and the smaller Sukama airfield to the west of the island, and Ishigaki had the one large airfield.

From early morning on the 3rd April the carriers of Task Group 58.1 started to launch their aircraft, with Hellcats from USS *Belleau Wood* CVL-24 strafing Sukama airfield runway and buildings close by with its machine guns and rockets. The one aircraft seen in a revetment was attacked, but did not explode or catch fire and the pilots thought that this aircraft could possibly be a dummy or an aircraft that had been written off.

Revetments were basically embankments with a supporting facing wall that were built to protect aircraft on the ground against bombing and strafing attacks. The Japanese, however, would use these revetments as a trap for the attacking aircraft by surrounding the revetments with camouflaged Anti-Aircraft sites and have dummy aircraft inside the revetment. Their aim was to draw the attacking aircraft in and then hit them with intensive AA fire, which in most cases brought the aircraft down.

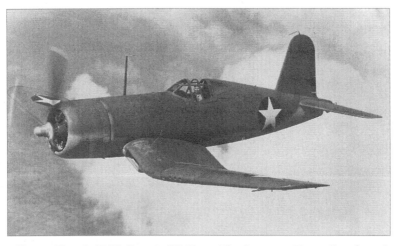

Chance Vought F4U Corsair US Navy. The Japanese Zero pilots feared being attacked by the Corsair, which they named 'Whistling Death'.
Jacques Trempe Collection

Grumman Hellcat F6F F-36.   Jacques Trempe Collection

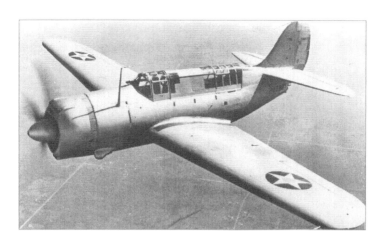

Curtiss Helldiver -2819 XSBC-1 (1784) prototype.
Made first flight 18th December 1940. Ron Dupas Collection
This aircraft first crashed due to engine failure on landing 8th February, 1941. It
crashed again on 21st December 1941 due to wing failure during a test dive,
but this time destroyed.

USS *Bennington* CV-20 had launched her Hellcats, Corsairs, Helldivers and Avengers to strafe and bomb Norbara airfield, and USS *Hornet* CV-12 had launched her Hellcats, Helldivers and Avengers for an attack on Hirara airfield, with attacks also on craft on the water and towns and starting fires. Some Hellcats were tasked to take photographs of the damage on the airfields and the island. These attacks were repeated by the carrier aircraft continuously during the day, giving the Japanese little respite. Hellcat fighters were launched from USS *Hornet* CV-12, along with fighters from the other carriers, to bomb an airfield that had been reported to be being constructed, but when the fighters arrived it was seen that the work had been stopped. The fighters flew over the island and destroyed a number of boats and some small merchant ships anchored off shore, while other facilities on shore were strafed. Further sweeps of the smaller islands by fighters were undertaken to see if there were any military sites that needed dealing with, but the main Japanese strengths appeared to be on Miyako and Ishigaki.

Damage was sustained to aircraft on the ground at Hirara airfield and the runways were well cratered by the Helldiver bombers and Avenger torpedo bombers. At the end of the day the people on Miyako and Ishigaki knew that the Allies meant business, but it was just a beginning. The military were caught off guard by the aircraft from Task Group 38.1 who were able to attack with very little Anti-Aircraft return fire, but it was doubtful whether the Japanese would allow themselves to be in such a position in the future.

Following the attacks by Task Group 58.1 on the 3rd April, Task Group 38.4 also attacked the Sakishima Gunto on the 5th April. The Task Group was joined by the light cruiser USS *Oakland* CL-95, which had been in San Francisco in January 1945 for repairs, departing on the 4th March. After calling at Pearl Harbour she sailed for Ulithi, leaving there on the 31st March to join TG 38.4, where she joined in the strike on the Sakishima Gunto on the 5th April.

CHAPTER 18

Operation Ten-Go, from 6-7 April, 1945

In advance of the planned invasion of the Japanese mainland, American forces invaded Okinawa on 1st April 1945. The Imperial Japanese Navy's response was to organise a mission codenamed 'Operation Ten-Go' that would see the commitment of much of IJN remaining surface fleet. This included the large battleship *Yamato,* the cruiser *Yahagi* and eight destroyers that would sail to Okinawa and, combined with the kamikaze and land based army aircraft units, attack the Allied forces assembled on and around Okinawa.

In preparation for the mission, the designated 'Surface Special Attack Force' ships left Tokuyama on the 6th April with only enough fuel for a one way trip. Unfortunately for the Japanese, the Americans were now intercepting and decoding their radio transmissions and were able to gain advance information of Operation Ten-Go. Further confirmation of Japanese intentions came around 20:00 hrs when the Surface Special Attack Force, navigating the Bungo Strait, was spotted by the American submarines USS *Threadfin* and *Hackleback.* Both reported *Yamato*'s position to the main American carrier strike force, but neither of the submarines could attack because of the speed of the Japanese ships.

Admiral Raymond Spruance, concerned that the invasion force would be attacked, ordered six of his battleships that were engaged in shore bombardment to prepare for action against *Yamato* and the other IJN warships, but these orders were changed to air strikes from Admiral Mitscher's Task Force 58 aircraft carriers. To further ensure the safety of the amphibious force, some battleships, along with cruisers and destroyers, were tasked to protect the amphibious craft from the Japanese fleet.

The aim of the battleship *Yamato,* light cruiser *Yahagi* and the eight destroyers was to fight their way through the American fleet and all deliberately sail on to the Okinawa beaches. They would then act as shore batteries until they were put out of action. The crew would then disembark and become foot soldiers fighting alongside the Japanese Army. This was in fact a form of kamikaze operation, but instead of using aircraft they were using what was left of their surface warships.

The aircraft from Vice Admiral Mitscher's Task Force 58 sighted the battleship *Yamoto* just after midday and the attacks from the US fighters, dive bombers and torpedo bombers started. The cruiser *Yahagi* was seriously damaged when the first torpedo hit her, striking the engine room and leaving the vessel without power. More torpedoes and bombs hit the *Yahagi* and she began to sink.

The battleship *Yamoto* was also hit by torpedoes and bombs, and started to list to port. The commander of Operation Ten-Go, Vice Admiral Ito, saw the *Yamoto* was going to sink and ordered the crew to abandon ship. Shortly after the *Yamoto* capsized, there was a huge explosion which split the hull open and she began to sink.

USS *Randolph*, which had been refuelling on the 7th April, re-joined Task Group 58.2 and took part in the battle.

Grumman F6F Hellcats 74 and 72 from VF-12 Squadron on USS Randolph.
(Note the wooden flight deck).   *Ray Crupi Collection*

Operation Ten-Go made very little difference to the Okinawa invasion, with only small losses of American aircraft compared to the IJN losses, which included the destroyer *Yamoto*, cruiser *Yahagi* and four other destroyers, and the huge cost to life of over 4,000 IJN sailors. This was effectively the end of Imperial Japanese Navy as a powerful fighting force, and with the end of the war in sight, the remaining IJN warships would not cause the Allied fleet any further serious trouble.

Task Force 57 strikes on Sakishima Gunto from the 6-7 April

While Operation Ten-Go was ongoing, Task Force 57 returned to attacks on the Sakishima Gunto on the 6th April. It was believed that the Japanese may be flying aircraft off in the early hours of the morning from the Ishigaki and Miyako airfields after the runways had been repaired from the previous days cratering by the allied strikes. At 04.50hrs four fighters flew off HMS *Indomitable* with two going to Miyako and the other two to Ishigaki to see if any aircraft were taking off. If aircraft were seen, the fighters would attack and destroy them, but no aircraft were seen. It was observed that the runways on Miyako had been repaired overnight, and Avengers were tasked to bomb the runways again and re-crater them. While the Avengers bombed the airfields on Miyako, the fighters attacked radio and radar stations, and also sank some craft on the water. On the return from Miyako, Hellcats from 1844 Squadron came across a Frances (torpedo bomber) to which they gave chase until it was shot down.

In the afternoon there was an Avenger strike, but due to an accident on board HMS *Victorious*, 3 Avengers were unable to take-off and one 849 Squadron Avenger ditched in the sea just after taking off. Japanese Judys were detected and attacked, to be dealt with by the Corsairs and Hellcats, which shot down one Judy while another dived on HMS *Illustrious* and missed. Of the other Japanese aircraft, one Jill was shot down by Corsairs and another Judy by Corsairs and Hellcats. However, sadly one Seafire was shot down by friendly fire, with the loss of the pilot, and two Corsairs were destroyed by enemy bombs.

163

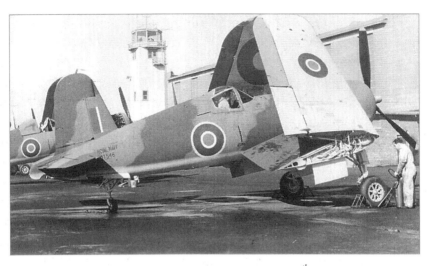

British Corsairs: V-166 Mk II Corsair RN JT546. On 6th April 1945 flown by
Sub. Lt. (A) G. S. P. Salmon RNVR shared claim on shooting down
a Japanese Judy.   Bill Pippin Collection

The BPF Task Force 57 resumed attacks on Sakishima Gunto on the 7th April, and in the early morning sweeps the fighters reported that all the runways on the Miyako and Ishigaki airfields had been repaired, and so three bombing strikes were made again on the runways of the airfields to again put them out of action, while the fighters strafed military installations and shipping. At the end of the day, two Avengers were shot down and three Corsairs were lost, while the Japanese lost five aircraft which were shot down and three aircraft shot up on the ground.

Task Force 57 then left to refuel at Area Cootie on 8th April, which was the American refuelling area, but was closer than Midge or Mosquito. HMCS *Uganda*, HMS *Urchin* and HMS *Ursa* joined, and RNZN *Gambia* re-joined after towing HMS *Ulster* to Leyte. The final strikes on the Sakishima Gunto were planned for the 9th and 10th April before the task force left for Leyte.

Intense Kamikaze strikes on American Fleet

While the British Task Force 57 had some initial experience of the kamikaze attacks, the US Fleet had been seriously battered by massed attacks from kamikaze suicide aircraft as well as conventional bombing attacks and had received significant damage to their warships.

The problems that the kamikaze fighters were causing to the American seaborne fleet were of great concern to Admiral Spruance and he requested that the British Pacific Fleet Task Force 57 broke away from their planned attacks on Sakishima Gunto before returning to Leyte, to concentrate on attacks against the airfields of Shinchiku and Matsuyama on Northern Formosa (Operation Iceberg Oolong). As well as the Japanese using the Sakishima Gunto as staging posts for aircraft to transfer to Okinawa, Admiral Spruance believed that many of the kamikaze aircraft were originating from there and using the islands as flying off bases, and he wanted the airfields on Formosa dealt with.

While Task Force 57 was refuelling at Area Cootie it was agreed between the British and American Commanders that the BPF would disengage from the Sakishima attacks, to deal with the Formosa airfields before their return to Leyte.

US Task Group 52.1 Support Carrier Group

While the British Task Force 57 was away from the Sakishima Gunto on the Formosa mission, the responsibility of sustaining the attacks on the islands was passed to Rear Admiral Calvin T. Durgin's Task Group 52.1 Support Carrier Group of the American Fifth Fleet. The group was made up of escort carriers, destroyers and destroyer escorts. The escort carriers were smaller than the fleet carriers and carried Avenger Torpedo Bombers and Wildcat fighters. The Carrier Support Group operated with three Task Units, 52.1.1, 52.1.2 and 52.1.3, and from the 8th April until the 12th April, TU 52.1.3 took over from Task Force 57 while they were on their Formosa mission.

Task Unit 52.1.3 was under the command of Rear Admiral William Sample and consisted of the escort carriers:

USS *Suwannee*: CVE-27 F6F Hellcats (VF-40), TBM Avengers (VT-40)

USS *Sangamon*: CVE-26 F6F Hellcats (VF-33), TBM Avengers (VT-33)

USS *Chenango*: CVE-28 F6F Hellcats (VF-25), TBM Avengers (VT-25)

USS *Santee*: CVE-29 F6F Hellcats (VF-24), TBM Avengers (VT-24)

The Task Group received cover from 6 Destroyers and 8 Destroyer Escorts.

From the 8th April, strikes were made against Ishigaki and Miyako by aircraft from the USS *Suwannee* and USS *Santee*, escort carriers of TU 52.1.3, concentrating at first on Hirara airfield on Miyako, where the AA positions were strafed and rocketed by the Hellcats and aircraft were destroyed on the ground. The bombing of the airfield and cratering of the runways was conducted by the Avengers.

After the first strike on Miyako, USS *Sangamon* sent fighters and bombers to Ishigaki, and along with Hellcats and Avengers from USS *Chenango*, attacked the runways, revetments and AA positions on Ishigaki airfield. The next day similar attacks continued on Miyako and Ishigaki, continuing the harassment to the islands and the airfields. However, an accident happened to USS *Chenango* when a Hellcat was landing and its tail hook broke after hooking on to the arrester wire, missing the barrier and careering into parked aircraft, destroying seven planes. Fires erupted from the fuel in the aircraft, but further damage was avoided by the carrier changing course. USS *Chenango* was out of action for a short time while the decks were cleaned up.

Attacks continued against Ishigaki and Miyako on the 10th April, causing further damage on Miyako when attacks on Norbara hit a storage tank and a radar installation, as well as aircraft on the ground. On this day, due to USS *Suwannee* leaving for Kerama Retto for replenishment, Rear Admiral Sample changed his flag to USS *Sangamon*. Kerama Retto was near Okinawa and was used as the supply base for the four escort carriers. While USS *Suwannee* was away, further attacks were launched on the islands to maintain the constant pressure on Ishigaki and Miyako.

Grumman Wildcat F4F-F US Navy (known as the Martlet in the British Royal Navy).   Jacques Trempe Collection

TU52. 1.2 under the command of Rear Admiral Felix B. Stump:

USS *Marcus Island* CVE-77   Wildcats and Avengers (VC-87)
USS *Saginaw Bay* CVE-82   Wildcats and Avengers (VC-88)
USS *Sargent Bay* CVE-83   Wildcats and Avengers (VC-83)
USS *Petrof Bay* CVE-80   Wildcats and Avengers (VC-93)
USS *Rudyerd Bay* CVE-81   Wildcats and Avengers (VC-96)
USS *Tulagi* CVE-72   Wildcats and Avengers (VC-92)
USS *Makasser Strait* CVE-91 Wildcats and Avengers (VC-97)

The Escort Carriers of TU52.1.2 were the 'Casablanca Class' with two lifts and a catapult, and could fly the later type of Wildcat F2 fighters. Rear Admiral Stump, USN, was commanding TU52.1.2 from his flagship *USS Marcus Island* CVE-77, with his second in command Rear Admiral Henderson, USN in USS *Saginaw Bay* CVE-82.

USS *Makassar* Strait CVE-91

USS *Makassar Strait* CVE-91 had left Pearl Harbour on the 29th January, 1945, after embarking Squadron VC-97 for combat duties in the western Pacific. After joining Task Group 50.8 on 9th February 1945, USS *Makasser Strait* CVE-91was first engaged in cover for the US Fleet from fierce Japanese air strikes from the ongoing Battle of Iwo Jima, in the Bonin Islands, a group of volcanic islands that was a stronghold of the Japanese military. It was off Chichi Jima, the largest Bonin Island, that the future American President George H. W. Bush, aged 20, crashed and was rescued by an American submarine.

After leaving the Bonin Islands, USS *Makasser Strait* left for the Ryukyus Islands and joined Task Unit 52.1.2 on the 8th April 1945, to take part in air support operations. The carrier's VC-97 TMB-3 aircraft were then engaged in strikes in the Ryukyus for the next month, in support of the American troop landings.

A member of the Composite Squadron VC-97 on board the USS *Makasser Strait* was Lt. Vernon L. Tebo, who was the pilot of one of the TBM-3 Avengers, with his crew Warren N. Loyd and Robert Tuggle Junior. Lt. Vernon Tebo was the first flying instructor that Sub. Lt. Geoffrey Wright had at Grosse Ile, Detroit, whom he held in high regard and remembered very fondly for his excellent training and his fun attitude.

TU 52.1.2 take over from TU 52.1.3

Rear Admiral Sample's Task Unit 52.1.3 was relieved on the 13th April by Rear Admiral Stump's TU 52.1.2, while TU 52.1.3 sailed to the south east of Okinawa.

Avengers and Wildcats from the USS *Makasser Strait* and USS *Tulagi* made strikes on the three airfields of Hirara, Nobara and Sukama, on Miyako, with the Wildcats strafing and rocketing the runways, followed by bombing from the Avengers, and ground aircraft were hit. Although the AA appeared to be light, still one Wildcat was shot down and another damaged by flak. USS *Petrof Bay*, USS *Marcus Bay* and USS *Rudyerd Bay* made strikes on Ishigaki and Miyayo airfield and although two US fighters were shot down, their pilots were rescued. The next day TU 52.1.2 continued with their attacks on Ishigaki and Miyako and seven aircraft were destroyed with 25 damaged on the ground, along with the loss of some US aircraft. On the 15th April, aircraft from TU52.1.2 started their strikes from early morning, on Ishigaki and Miyako, but this was the day that Lt. Vernon Tebo and his crew were shot down over Ishigaki airfield.

Lt. Vernon Tebo and his crew are lost

Lt. Tebo, aged 28, and his crew, Aviation Ordnance man 1st Class Robert Tuggle Jr., aged 20, and Aviation Radioman 1st Class Warren H. Loyd, aged 24, took off in a TBF Avenger from the USS *Makassar Strait* for a reconnaissance mission over Ishigaki Island on the 15th April 1945. With the heavy Japanese Anti-Aircraft fire the TBF was hit and the crew were forced to parachute from the plane. They landed in the sea and swam to a coral reef, but were captured by Japanese sailors. At first they were interrogated and tortured, and finally Lt. Tebo and Robert Tuggle Jr were decapitated, but Warren H. Loyd was used for bayonet practice by the Japanese military. The injuries he received from the constant stabbing of the bayonets killed him. These horrific war crimes were in violation of the Geneva Convention signed in 1929, and were not to go unpunished. After the war, over 40 Japanese soldiers and sailors who were involved in the capture, torture, beheading and bayoneting, were convicted on war crime charges. Seven who were most directly involved in the killings, were executed by hanging.

L-R Robert Tuggle Jnr, Lt. Tebo and Warren Loyd
Courtesy of John B. Tuggle www.ShipleyBay.com

By the end of the 15th April, the results of the strikes on Ishigaki and Miyako left the Ishigaki airfield runways well cratered, as were the Hirara and Sukama airfields on Miyako. However, the American reconnaissance of Nobara airfield seemed to indicate that that the runways could still be used. USS *Makassar Strait*, with USS *Dennis* as Destroyer escort left that evening for Kerama Retto for re-supply.

While TU.52.1.2 were engaged in strikes on the Sakishima Islands, Sub. Lt. Wright was with Task Force 57 for the strikes on Formosa, and had no idea that Lt. Tebo was engaged in combat duties in the Sakishima Gunto at the same time, and only learned of the fate of Lt. Tebo in 2011.

Operation Kikusui from 6 April-22 June, 1945

During the Okinawa campaign, the Japanese leadership planned a special attack mission code named 'Operation Kikusui' ('Floating Chrysanthemum') that was to last from the 6th April to the 22nd June, 1945. The 'Floating Chrysanthemum' was the emblem of a 14th century Japanese warrior, who in the moments before defeat in a battle chose to commit ritual suicide rather than be captured.

The operation was aimed to attack the American Navy warships with up to 1,500 kamikaze aircraft in a series of ten attacks, including the first Ohka rocket planes carried by Betty bombers, one of which sank the American destroyer USS *Mannert L. Abele.* The result of the Kikusui attacks was a huge loss to the American ships and sailors, but the Japanese, despite causing so much damage to the American fleet, finished up with a massive loss of their own aircraft and pilots.

From the Kikusui 1 on the 6th to 7th April when 355 kamikaze aircraft were involved in the attacks to a reduction to 145 kamikaze aircraft in Kikusui 2 on the 11th to 13th April, shows how there was quite a loss in the first attacks. By the last two day Kikusui 9 from the 3rd to 7th June with just 50 kamikaze aircraft, and Kikusui 10 from 21st to 22nd June of 45 kamikaze aircraft involved in the attacks, demonstrates the huge number of Japanese kamikaze aircraft and suicide pilots that had been lost.

170

The effect on the American sailors' morale was quite devastating through the number of attacks by the Japanese aircraft, but also from the 24 hour watches that had to be mounted for possible attacks at any time. By the end of the campaign most of the kamikaze aircraft approaching the American fleet were quickly shot down or had to turn back.

CHAPTER 19

Operation Iceberg Oolong and return to Sakishima Gunto

HMS *Indomitable* and HMS *Indefatigable* were tasked for 'Operation Iceberg Oolong', the attacks on Formosa between the 9th April and 16th April, when Task Force 57 returned to their attacks on the Sakishima Islands. For the attacks on Formosa arrangements were made for an American 'Dumbo' (ASR Catalina Flying Boat) to be available with fighter cover to pick up any pilots and crew that ditched in the sea.

On the 11th April Task Force 57 was in their flying off positions but the weather over the target area was not good and the attacks were held up until the 12th April when the weather had improved enough for two escorted Avenger strikes. Strike 1 was 620 Squadron and 857 Squadron, and Strike 2 was for 849 Squadron and 854 Squadron, but one Avenger from 849 Squadron was shot down with the loss of the crew. Two Fireflies from 1770 Squadron shot down four Sonia's and damaged another, while Seafires from HMS *Indefatigable* shot down one Zeke from a flight of four.

Damaged aircraft were dumped over the side. Courtesy of Paul Whiteing

Other successes were of Corsairs shooting down a Dinah, but another Dinah and 2 Oscars managed to escape, one Hellcat dealt with a Zeke and 3 Hellcats shot down 4 Oscars and a Tony. Corsairs also shot down a Val and an Oscar. One Hellcat was damaged and crash landed with the loss of the pilot, and a Corsair was forced to ditch, also with the loss of the pilot.

The strike on Shinchiku airfield was strongly defended by Anti-Aircraft positions maintaining heavy flak coverage. Due to cloud cover over Matsuyama airfield the planned strike was diverted to a secondary target at Kiirun harbour, where the docks, shipping and a chemical plant were hit, and targets in the surrounding area of Matsuyama airfield were identified and attacked. The Japanese responded by sending aircraft to attack the fleet, but the CAP of Hellcats and Corsairs dealt with them.

The weather on the 13th April was much better over Matsuyama airfield, and strikes were made on both Matsuyama and Shinchiku airfields causing damage to aircraft on the ground, runways, hangers, barracks, a railway bridge and a train, as well as other targets destroyed, with no loss to the aircraft from the carriers. However, earlier in the morning when it was just getting light, HMS *Indomitable* had a lucky escape when a 'Val' (Navy dive bomber), pretending to be US fighter, dropped a bomb, which fortunately bounced off the flight deck and into the sea. This aircraft got away, but the following Val was not so lucky and was hit soundly by the anti-aircraft fire and crashed. A flight of four Hellcats was ordered to 'keep clear', but one was shot down by the same guns when it strayed into their line of fire. A second group of enemy aircraft that attacked the British Pacific Fleet and were intercepted by Corsairs, with two Zekes also shot down.

It was while the British aircraft were engaged in attacks on Formosa that they also came across a variety of other Japanese aircraft. As well as the Val Navy dive bombers, they engaged with other bombers, including the Sonia (Army Bomber), Sally (Army bomber), Oscar (Army fighter), Tojo (Army fighter), Zeke (Navy fighter) and Tony (Army fighter).

Due to the heavy attacks on the American Forces in Okinawa

173

and the use of the Sakishima Gunto islands as staging posts for the kamikaze aircraft from Formosa to Okinawa, the British Pacific Fleet offered to delay its return to Leyte for replenishment and continue their strikes on the Sakishima Gunto. This offer was welcomed and appreciated by the Americans. The Task Force then sailed for Area Cootie for refuelling on the 14th April, when HMS *Formidable* joined Task Force 57, replacing HMS *Illustrious*, which then sailed for Leyte.

The American and British Fleets heard that the President of the United States, Franklin D. Roosevelt, had died on the 12th April, and all the ships had their flags flying at half-mast while at sea.

British Pacific Fleet Task Force 57 return to the Sakishima Gunto

Task Force 57 set sail again on the 15th April to the flying off point in the Sakishima area, and on the 16th April the aircraft undertook further strikes on Ishigaki, beginning at 06.30 and 12.30, which rendered the airfields as unusable, and Miyako was attacked at 09.30 and 15.30, also putting their airfields out of action. During the attack on Miyako, rocket-firing Fireflies strafed buildings, installations and aircraft on the ground. However, the Japanese were well prepared in their defence of their airfields and laid traps, consisting of dummy or real aircraft that had been written off, which from the air deceived the attacking pilots. The danger for the strike aircraft was that the dummy aircraft were positioned within the flak area and the pilots were greeted by a heavy barrage of flak, which brought down a number of the Fleet Air Arm aircraft.

On the 17th April, reconnaissance showed that the runways had been repaired on Miyako, but not on Ishigaki, so the first of three strikes was made on Miyako starting at 06.30 hours. In the final strike, one Avenger was shot down and ditched in the sea just off the town of Hirara, but the skilled rescue operations undertaken by the Walrus amphibians was demonstrated when the crew of the Avenger was rescued. While the rescue was ongoing, the fighter cover dealt with the firing coming from Hirara. One Myrt was shot down by Hellcats from 1844 Squadron, one Corsair from 1836 Squadron shot down a Zeke, and the Hellcats shot down 2 Zekes.

An example of the loss of aircraft and crew from one aircraft carrier in Task Force 57 can be illustrated by HMS *Victorious*, which had left Ulithi with 43 Corsair pilots and 17 Avenger crews, but was then down to 31 Corsair pilots and 14 Avenger crews that were fit for flying. Task Force 57 then left for the refuelling area from 18th to 19th April.

There was a change in Task Units with Rear Admiral Sample's TU 52.1.3 replacing Rear Admiral Stump's TU 52.1.2 for the strikes on Sakishima Gunto on the 18th to 19th April.

Continuous attacks were made on Sakishima Gunto on the 19th to 20th April, with USS *Sangamon* launching her Hellcats, Wildcats and Avengers for strikes on Ishigaki and Miyako, while USS *Chanango*, USS *Santee* and USS *Suwannee* also attacking the airfields with their Hellcats and Avengers and providing CAP and anti-submarine patrols. The strikes focused on cratering the runways, destroying aircraft in revetments, and Anti-Aircraft positions, including surrounding buildings on the airfields which were set on fire. One of the problems found with the Japanese AA fire was that there was no visual tracer seen coming up and the fact that the ammunition they were using tended to be without a flash when fired from an AA gun. Without the flash the pilot may not know he was being fired at, or even be aware if his aircraft had been hit. This was quite dangerous, especially if a pilot thought he was attacking an aircraft in a revetment, which could be a dummy, and fell into the trap of being hit by heavy ground fire which could bring him down.

When Task Force 57 returned on the 20th April, and for just the one day they continued with strafing and bombing to further crater the runways of Miyako and Ishigaki airfields, which had been repaired overnight, while the fighters maintained CAP over the airfields to deter the Japanese from attempting any repairs of the runways. One Avenger from 848 Squadron ditched in the sea, but the pilot was rescued by the US Dumbo.

Later in the day Task Force 57 set sail for Leyte to undergo maintenance and resupply, arriving on the 23rd April after completing 32 days at sea. The Task Force had lost 19 aircraft to flak and a further 28 aircraft operationally, with 16 pilots killed and 13 aircrew killed or missing. The Task Force anchored in San Pedro Bay, Leyte, close to the Fleet Train, where the repairs and replenishment of the ships started and continued for the remainder of the week, with the battle damage to HMS *Formidable* taking six days to repair.

For the period from the 21st April to the 3rd May, while the British Pacific Fleet Task Force 57 was in Leyte, Rear Admiral Sample's TU 52.1.3 was tasked to maintain the continuous strikes on the Sakishima Gunto. However, while TU 52.1.3 went for refuelling and replenishment on the 28th April, TU 52.1.1 was to replace them for attacks on the Sakishima Gunto.

This period for Rear Admiral Sample's TU 52.1.3 was not to be 2 days action and 2 days refuelling and replenishment that had been the arrangements with the British Pacific Fleet Task Force 57.

To manage the refuelling, rearming and supply, TU 52.1.3 would release one carrier at a time, with an escort of destroyers, to go to Kerama Retto for replenishment and return within two days. This went on until the 28th April, when for one day all the carriers from TU 52.1.3 went for refuelling and replenishment while TU 52.1.1 took over the strikes on Sakishima Gunto.

TU 52.1.1

USS *Makin Island* was the flagship of Rear Admiral Calvin T. Durgin.

USN as USS *Makin Island* CVE-93 Wildcats and Avengers (VC-84)

USS *Fanshaw Bay* CVE-70 Wildcats and Avengers (VC-68)

USS *Shamrock Bay* CVE-84 Wildcats and Avengers (VC-94)

USS *Savo Island* CVE 78   Wildcats and Avengers (VC-91)

USS *Steamer Bay* CVE-87 Wildcats and Avengers (VC-90)

Kerama Retto Supply and Replenishment Base

Kerama Retto was 15 miles west of Okinawa, and in advance of the Okinawa landings, there was a need to capture advance bases and anchorages. This started on the 24th March 1945, when aircraft from Task Force 58 commenced strikes on the Kerama Retto islands anti-aircraft positions, beach and coastal defences, including military installations, and also covered the mine sweepers clearing the approaches to the beaches. This was prior to the invasion beaches being checked on the next day for obstacles and traps set by the Japanese. Once the beaches were cleared, the US Army forces were free to land on the islands. The US Forces achieved their aim and the Kerama Retto islands were occupied by the Americans before the Okinawa landings started on the 1st April 1945.

During the attack on Kerama Retto, the US forces were able to find and destroy a large number of well-camouflaged suicide motor boats, known as the IJN Shino EMBs (Explosive Motor Boats). Also captured, along with an excellent re-supply anchorage, was a Japanese seaplane base, to be then used by the US for anti-submarine patrols.

After being in control of the Kerama Retto for just over a month, the supply anchorage became well known by the American sailors as 'Suicide Alley'. This was because of the number of massed kamikaze attacks that flew over and attacked the ships.

USS *Sangamon* from TU 52.1.3 was to experience attacks by kamikaze suicide aircraft after arriving at Kerama Retto with her two escort destroyers on the 3rd May 1945. After anchoring, the work of replenishment started and during the day there were many alerts for kamikaze attacks. The carrier had completed her replenishment and had just started to leave to return to the Sakishima Gunto, when an unidentified aircraft was detected and fighters were sent up to intercept. One Japanese aircraft, a Tony (Army Ki 61 fighter) that had got through, dived on USS *Sangamon*, but missed and went in the sea. However, later on one Japanese Nick (Army Ki 45 twin engine fighter) was sighted and maintained its flight through the AA from the ships and dived on to the flight deck. The crash of the aircraft, combined with the exploding bomb, caused fires on deck and also in the hanger deck, destroying and damaging aircraft. The attack resulted in a large number of crew casualties. The damage to the carrier was severe enough to warrant time in a naval dockyard for repairs.

Important decisions on the future deployment of the British Pacific Fleet

While in Leyte, decisions on the future of the British Pacific Fleet were considered by Admiral Rawlings who was in discussions with American Commanders on board HMS *King George V*. One of the considerations preferred by the American Commanders was for Task Force 57 to disengage from Operation Iceberg and take part in a Borneo operation. However, the final decision was communicated by Admiral Nimitz on the 27th April, when he stated that the British Pacific Fleet was to continue with Operation Iceberg, which was the preferred option of Admiral Rawlings. The plan was to leave Leyte on the 1st May and return to the Sakishima Gunto for a period of up to four weeks and complete a cycle of combat strikes over two days and withdrawal to the replenishment areas for two days. The American Task Units would, as before, then take over during the British Task Force replenishment breaks to maintain the regular attacks on the Sakishima islands.

The Fleet Destroyer HMS *Quilliam* arrived at Leyte from Sydney on the 28th April to join Task Force 57, and just two days later the replenishment of the Task Force was completed. To be in position for refuelling Task Force 57 en-route, the tanker group left Leyte, escorted by the 7th Destroyer Flotilla, consisting of HMAS *Napier* (D7 CO, Captain Herbert Buchanan), HMAS *Nepal*, HMAS *Norman* and HMAS *Nizam*.

Orders had been issued for Task Force 57 to sail on the 1st May for Sakishima Gunto, to continue with Operation Iceberg. The Task Force was to include the 1st Battle Squadron, 1st Carrier Squadron, 4th Cruiser Squadron, 25th Destroyer Flotilla, 4th Destroyer Flotilla and 27th Destroyer Flotilla.

HM Ships not joining Task Force 57 were HMS *Illustrious*, HMS *Argonaut*, *Wager* and *Whelp*, which were to sail from Leyte to Sidney on the 4th May for refit. HMS *Formidable* was to take the place of HMS *Illustrious* with Task Force 57 while she was in Sydney.

With the first strikes scheduled for the 4th May, Sub. Lt. Wright was to take to the air on the 2nd May while HMS *Indomitable* was at sea:

'I took off solo in TBM JZ634 for a practice flight where I practised stalls and two deck landings in preparation for joining 857 Squadron for their attacks on the airfields of Sakishima Gunto.'

On the 3rd May refuelling was undertaken in Area Mosquito, with Task Force 57 of the British Pacific Fleet arriving back off the Sakishima Gunto after replenishment by the 4th May.

CHAPTER 20

Operation Iceberg Two

Bombardment of the airfields on Miyako

One of the aims was to use some of the battleships and cruisers, screened by destroyers as a bombarding force, to target and suppress the AA defences on the Miyako airfields. The vessels involved were the battleships HMS *King George V* and HMS *Howe*, screened by the 25th Destroyer Flotilla, cruisers HMS *Euryalus*, *Swiftsure*, HMNZS *Gambia* and HMCS *Uganda*. Once in position at 12.05 they opened fire with HMS *King George V* and *Howe* bombarding the runways, buildings and AA defences on Hirara airfield, while HMS *Euryalus* and *Black Prince* concentrated on 'air bursts' over the AA defences on Norbara airfield. HMS *Swiftsure* and HMNZS *Gambia* continued shelling Norbara airfield while HMCS *Uganda* concentrated on the Sukama airstrip. The carriers were tasked to provide CAP for the bombardment operation, but while the bombardment was going on, the kamikaze attacks were getting through and diving on the aircraft carriers. Both HMS *Formidable* and HMS *Indomitable* had kamikaze strikes.

The destroyers that were screening the bombardment force hastily returned to protect the carriers from the kamakaze attacks. The Japanese had other fighters in the air as well as the kamikaze aircraft, some of which were escort fighters for the kamikaze fighters. The aim of these aircraft was to draw the British fighters from the kamikaze aircraft, by climbing and attracting radar detection from carriers. This ruse was quite successful, as the kamikaze aircraft were only detected by the carriers when a Japanese plane was seen diving on HMS *Formidable*.

The aircraft that hit HMS *Formidable* was a Zeke (Zero) which struck its island, splitting open part of the armoured deck, causing a fire in the hanger below and the loss of 8 crew and 47 wounded. Also, a number of aircraft on the flight deck were damaged beyond repair.

Another Zeke flying across the flight deck of HMS *Indomitable* was fired upon by the carriers' 4.5. guns, but returned in a steep dive and on fire from the hits it had received from the guns of HMS *Indomitable* and also a nearby destroyer HMS *Quality,* while aiming for the flight deck of the carrier.

HMS Formidable under attack.   Courtesy of Paul Whiteing

Damage to the carrier.   Courtesy of Paul Whiteing

Damage to aircraft on deck.   Courtesy of Paul Whiteing

Damage to a Corsair   Courtesy of Paul Whiteing

HMS *Indomitable* was already turning sharply to avoid being hit and the Zeke struck a glancing blow on the flight deck before bouncing off into the sea where its bomb exploded in the water. The carrier received slight damage with no loss of crew. This was a good example of the British Pacific Fleet's concentration on practicing various manoeuvres to avoid being hit by kamikaze aircraft. Another example of the success of the avoidance procedures was undertaken by HMS *Victorious* when a kamikaze pilot dived towards the flight deck. The carrier immediately did an emergency turn and the wing of the aircraft touched the flight deck before landing in the sea, where its bomb also exploded. The armoured flight decks were proving themselves time and time again, with the carriers back in action and their aircraft taking off and landing in a short period after being attacked.

Kamikaze attack on HMS Indomitable 4ᵗʰ May 1945. Geoffrey Wright Collection

Aircraft from HMS *Formidable* already in the air were directed to land on other carriers while the repairs to the flight deck were undertaken and later she could receive some of her Corsairs back on board. Due to the loss of aircraft through attacks by the Japanese aircraft and the hanger fire, HMS *Formidable* was only able to provide CAP (Combat Air Patrols) for the Avenger strikes on the Sakishima Gunto.

Other Japanese aircraft were dealt with by the Fleet, and this included two aircraft shot down by fighters into the sea even before they reached the fleet, one Jill by Hellcats from HMS

Indomitable and one Val from the Seafires of HMS *Indefatigable*. Later in the afternoon, Corsairs from HMS *Illustrious* also dealt with a Judy. By late afternoon there was a build-up of Japanese aircraft, but the alertness of the British fighters dealt with them. The Seafires of HMS *Indefatigable* were very busy when they came across a flight of four Zekes and shot down three of them. One Avenger from 857 Squadron was hit and crashed into the sea with 2 of the 3 crew killed.

The continuing aim of Operation Iceberg was to maintain attacks on the airfields of the Sakishima Gunto to ensure they were put out of action by bombing runways, other facilities and buildings. Also it was to destroy anti-aircraft sites and then maintain CAP (Combat Air Patrols) over the islands, airfields and surrounding sea, to prevent the Japanese repairing the runways, but the Japanese would not give in to the damage to the airfields during the day and just went about repairing them at night.

While bombing strikes continued on the airfields and runways by the combat patrols, reconnaissance revealed that more aircraft were using Hirara and Ishigaki airfields, which appeared to show that the Japanese were transferring more aircraft and equipment to the Okinawa battle area. These airfields were attacked and it resulted in destroying a significant number of aircraft on the ground. The Japanese were quick to fill in the bomb craters and put the runways back in service, and despite constant attacks on the runways the Japanese continued to fill the craters in and then were attacked again and again.

The attacks on the airfields on Miyako and Ishigaki continued from the 5th May with American Dumbo as well as the submarines ready for rescue missions. The American Dumbo would search for airmen who had ditched in the sea, or seamen whose ship had gone down, radio the position, and the rescue might be from a nearby warship or even the flying boat landing and picking up the survivors. Some search and rescue missions were provided by a land-based bomber, which would drop a lifeboat, or by the PBM Mariner and the PBY Catalina flying boats. For the 5th May the daytime Dumbo aircraft was provided by Task Force 51 from 08.30-17.00.

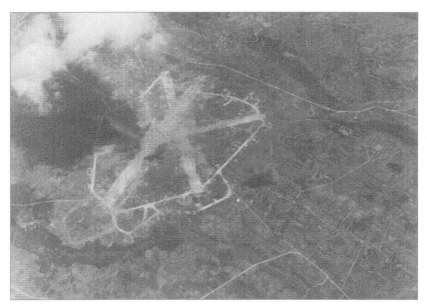

Hirara airfield attack.   *Frank Stockwell Collection*

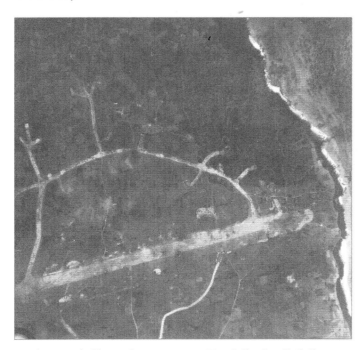

Nobara airfield attack.   *Frank Stockwell Collection*

Sub. Lt. Wright was involved in attacks on Miyako on the 5th and 6th May, but was pleased to return safely:

'I took off on the 5th May in TBM JZ624 with my crew, and we attacked Hirara airfield, Miyako, with 4 x 500lb bombs, followed by a strike on Nobara airfield the next day. The two attacks were successfully achieved, but we were very glad to get back to HMS *Indomitable* safely.'

The runways on the airfields were again cratered and put out of action, including aircraft destroyed on the ground. It was observed that little AA flak was coming up from the airfields, indicating that the ships bombardment had succeeded.

On the 6th May the fleet sailed out of the flying off area, for refuelling in Area Cootie, while the American Task Group 52.1 covered Sakishima. Replacement aircraft were also transferred from HMS *Striker* to make up for the losses on the carriers through action. As there was no hospital ship available, HMS *Striker* took on board injured seamen from HMS *Formidable* and left for Leyte, accompanied by HMS *Kempenfelt.*

While Task Force 57 retired for refuelling and replenishment on the 6th May, TU 52.1.3 took over. USS *Sangamon* had to go for repairs after being attacked by a kamikaze aircraft on the 4th May and she was replaced by USS *Block Island II* CVE 106. Action on the Sakishima Gunto was continued by USS *Suwannee* and USS *Chenango,* while USS *Block Island II* was acclimatised to the requirements for the strikes on the airfields of the islands. USS *Santee* was the carrier chosen to replenish at Kerama Retto, while the other carriers continued the strikes for the 6th to 7th May on Ishigaki and Miyako airfields, again cratering their runways, before pulling away for Task Force 57 to resume their attacks.

VC-97 Squadron transferred from USS *Makassar Strait* to USS *Shipley Bay*

On the 7th May, USS *Makassar Strait* CVE-91 transferred VC-97 'Fishhook' Squadron at Kerama Retto to USS *Shipley Bay* CVE-85 and left the same day for Guam, arriving on the 11th May, with her role to act as a support carrier for pilots taking part in refresher training on carriers operating between Guam and Saipan. She then departed for Hawaii on the 19th July, calling in at Kwajalein in the Marshall Islands to embark 50 aircraft, before reaching Pearl

Harbour on the 29th July. After embarking military passengers, she set sail from Pearl Harbour and sailed on the 14th August for the USA, arriving at San Diego on the 21st August 1945.

USS *Shipley Bay* had left Pearl Harbour on the 22nd April for Okinawa via Guam to join Task Group 52.1 and take part in her first combat operations starting on the 7th May on the Sakishima Gunto, but on the 16th May, while taking on fuel, some of her fuel tanks were damaged and she returned to Guam for repairs. From the 14th to 22nd June, USS *Shipley Bay* was again in back in action, with its aircraft attacking the airfields on Miyako and Ishigaki. After carrying out further attacks on the islands, USS *Shipley Bay* left the operating area and went for refitting at San Diego, where she remained to the end of the Pacific War.

While the American TU 52.1.3 were engaged on the Sakishima strikes, Task Force 57's replenishment continued on the 7th May, including transfer of mail and messages. Sub. Lt. Wright, with PO Scougall and PO Cowling, were part of the message deliveries and took off from HMS *Indomitable* to message drop on HMS *Formidable*. He also undertook a test flight in JZ592, where he found the propeller surging. Work was carried out on the damage to HMS *Formidable* and by the end of the day she was fully operational, and the Task Force left again for the flying off operation area for Sakishima attacks. It was later that evening that the fleet heard the news of the unconditional surrender of the German Forces to the Allied Forces, to take effect from one minute past midnight on the 9th May 1945.

The Fleet Train also left the replenishment area, with HMAS *Norman* escorting RFA *Wave King* and *Wave Monarch* to Leyte, while HMS *Whimbrel* and *Avon* escorted RFA *San Ambrosio*, *San Adolpho* and *Cedardale*.

Task Force 57 was in position at the flying off operational area on the 8th May for further attacks on Miyako and Ishigaki, combined with air patrols over the islands. The aim was to use the battleships and cruisers to bombard the Ishigaki runways and AA position, but the weather had deteriorated during the night and in the early hours of the morning the bombardment plan was dropped. The plan had been for the aircraft to carry out four strikes, which was the usual practice of two attacks on each island. The close air patrols took off in the early hours and reported on arrival over the islands that the weather was similar to that at sea, overcast and raining with poor visibility. The first strike was cancelled with the hope that the weather would improve. A study of meteorological charts showed that Formosa was experiencing similar weather and the monitoring by the air patrols over islands showed no improvement. It was therefore deduced that it would be unlikely with such weather conditions that the Japanese would attempt flying from Formosa via Miyako and Ishigaki islands, and the attacks for the day were cancelled.

The weather on the 9th May improved and although the plans for bombardment had been cancelled, the four Avenger strikes were to take part with two attacks on each island. The air patrols took off at 05.45 and once over the island, reported that the weather was suitable for flying. They also observed that the runways on Hirara airfield had been repaired and were in use.

Sub. Lt. Wright with his TAG crew (Telegraphist, Air-Gunner) in JZ624 was part of a strike on Miyara airfield, Ishigaki, where they bombed its runway and strafed buildings. However, the Japanese had a well-honed plan to draw aircraft away from their fighters, aiming for suicide attacks on the Fleet. This happened to a flight of Seafires, who were drawn away by one fighter which they shot down, but while they were engaged with the fighter, four kamikaze fighters, avoiding other patrol fighters, managed to climb to a height ready to start their dive on the fleet. By then the fleet was engaged in avoidance action from the attacks they knew were coming. HMS *Illustrious* was turning sharply, but a kamikaze fighter was already diving directly towards her flight deck. Although the fighter had been hit constantly by the carrier's AA fire, it crashed on to the deck, with its bomb exploding, holing the armoured deck and causing fires. The fires were quickly put out, but another kamikaze came across the stern of HMS *Illustrious* and well on fire from the gunners' hits, it glanced off the deck and went into the sea. The damage caused was to the flight deck with aircraft destroyed beyond repair on deck, and the casualties were three dead and nineteen injured.

Shortly after the damage to the carrier, another kamikaze appeared to be aiming for HMS *Illustrious*, but changed his mind and dived for the battleship HMS *Howe*. The aircraft was hit by gunfire so many times that he missed the battleship and dived into the sea in flames. This was followed a few minutes later by the fourth kamikaze aircraft that approached both HMS *Formidable* and HMS *Indomitable*, but finally crashed into HMS *Formidable* with a large explosion followed by fire, destroying six Corsairs and one Avenger on deck. This was not the end, because the explosion had caused a gap in the flight deck and burning petrol got into the hanger below, where other aircraft were damaged and all needed replacement. All these attacks occurred between 16.50 and 17.05, a period of 15 minutes. Within the hour HMS *Formidable* was fit to land aircraft again on its flight deck, but by that time had only 4 Avengers and 11 Corsairs that were serviceable. Due to the damage and losses to the carriers, the fleet withdrew for refuelling and replenishment at Area Cootie from the 10th to 11th May. Task Unit 52.1.3 was to again take over from Task Force 57 to maintain the pressure on the airfields of Miyako and Ishigaki.

The same pattern of strafing and bombing the airfields on Ishigaki and Miyako continued from USS *Chenango*, with aircraft from USS *Santee* supporting strikes on the airfields and for CAP. USS *Block Island II* CVE-106 joined TU 52.1.3, replacing USS *Sangaman* while she went for repairs after being damaged by a kamikaze suicide aircraft. USS *Block Island II* prepared to make her first strikes on Hirara and Nobara airfields with Corsairs and Hellcats fighters, while her TBM Avengers engaged on the bombing of the runways. During the attacks, one Avenger crashed with the loss of its crew, and another ditched in the sea with the crew rescued by an escort destroyer.

While TU 52.1.3 was engaged on strikes on the Sakishima Gunto, Task Force 57 was in Area Cootie on the 10th May for refuelling and replenishment of much needed aircraft, as well as the usual exchange of mail, messages and stores. After inspection of damage to HMS *Illustrious* and HMS *Formidable* the decision was made that the carriers could continue with operational strikes.

The replenishment continued on the 11th May and HMS *Kempenfelt* rejoined the Task Force from Leyte.

The American and British Task Groups had got used to the Japanese strategy of attacking from a height and diving steeply on the fleet vessels, but they then changed this strategy to low level attacks which were more difficult for the radar to pick up. The kamikaze pilots were accompanied by experienced pilots who flew with them to guide them to their targets. Once they were 20 miles from the target, the experienced pilots, who had been given enough fuel in their tanks to return to their base, would leave the suicide pilots, who only had enough fuel to reach their targets. The accompanying pilots' strategy would then be to climb and be picked up by the radar, which would draw air cover away from the fleet to investigation of the intruders, leaving the target area open for the low level attacking kamikaze aircraft.

The Fleet had to then plan for this type of attack, and the aim was to have HMS *Swiftsure*, HMS *Kempenfelt*, RCN *Uganda* and HMS *Wessex* as radar pickets stationed away from the fleet to give early warning of approaching enemy fighters. The Seafires were available on the 'jack patrols' to then deal with these aircraft. The cruisers HMS *Black Prince* and *Euryalus* were also part of the anti-aircraft screen, as well as one destroyer to sail to the stern of each carrier as protection.

Task Force 57 was back at their flying off positions on the 12th May, but the weather conditions were still overcast. While the early CAP flights took off, along with the first Avenger bombing strike, the usual two strikes on Ishigaki and two on Miyako were planned, but only one strike on Ishigaki was possible because of the weather. The runways on Miyara and Ishigaki had been repaired, but again the strike cratered the runways and other areas were strafed. Sub. Lt. Wright was engaged in attacking the runways on Ishigaki airfield and reported that only light flak was encountered.

Not to waste the opportunity, three strikes were made on Miyako and it was observed that both runways on Nobara airfield had been repaired and just one runway on Hirara, but the strike cratered the airfields again making them unusable. The other strikes on Miyako concentrated on buildings, installations and AA sites, causing fires and destroying aircraft on the ground.

A good example of the efficiency of the rescue services was seen that day, when the US Submarine, USS *Bluefish*, rescued an Avenger crew that had ditched after having engine trouble. The submarine was supported by the US 'Dumbo' rescue aircraft that took off from Keramo Retto to assist in directing the submarine to the aircrew's position, and the four Corsairs that provided air cover while the rescue took place. The US Dumbo also assisted in the rescue of another Avenger crew that had ditched, but had given the wrong coordinates for their position in the morning. Later in the afternoon, a flight of Fireflies were returning to the fleet and detected a flashing signal, which they proceeded to investigate. The ditched crew were signalling with a mirror, and a message was sent by the Fireflies given their correct position, to which HMS *Kempenfelt* was dispatched to rescue the crew. The US 'Dumbo' was responsible for guiding the destroyer to the crew's position and for their rescue.

The next day, May 13th, the early CAP flights reported that work had been ongoing all night repairing the runways on Miyako and Ishigaki, and the same plan of one attack on Ishigaki and three on Miyako airfields took place with all runways put out of action. Buildings were strafed and oil tanks set on fire on Miyako and similar on Ishigaki, with in addition storage areas and two radio stations being set on fire. As a result of a tummy bug causing sickness to a large number of aircrews on HMS *Indefatigable*, few aircraft were able to take part in the strikes, but aircraft from the other carriers went ahead with them.

At the end of the day, operations ceased and Task Force 57 withdrew to Area Cootie for refuelling and replenishment, while the Sakishima islands attacks were continued by the US Task Unit 52.1.3

The American Task Unit 52.1.3 returned to take over from Task Force 57 for the 14th to 15th May, and during that time the fighters engaged in strafing small boats around the coast, returning to do the same to the airfields on Miyako, along with the cratering of the airfields by the Avengers. The AA was intense and one

Avenger was shot down and ditched in the sea close to the town of Ishigaki, but shortly after the crew was rescued by a 'Dumbo' ASR plane.

Meanwhile, on the 14th May Task Force 57 was engaged in refuelling and replenishment of supplies, ammunition and transfer of aircraft from HMS *Striker,* the escort carrier that had been tasked to take the injured from HMS *Formidable* back to Leyte on May 6th. However, this time, following the request by the Commander for a hospital ship to be available, the hospital ship *Tjitjalengka* was in a waiting area and an aircraft was sent to direct the hospital ship to the refuelling area, where the injured were then transferred by a destroyer to *Tjitjalengka.*

On May 15th Sub. Lt. Wright in TBM FN852 was engaged in transfer of aircraft, taking Sub. Lt. Hunt to HMS *Striker* for transfer of replacement aircraft and to embark damaged aircraft, returning later to HMS *Indomitable.*

The Task Force left the refuelling and replenishment area and returned to the flying off area to continue its attacks on the Sakishima islands. The early morning flights took off with the first bombing strike, but an extra strike was added for that day and included three strikes on Miyako and two on Ishigaki. Sub. Lt. Wright was tasked for Ishigaki airfield and engaged with his TAG crew for strike on the E-W runway of Ishigaki Airfield:

'The anti-aircraft fire was very fierce, causing damage to a number of our aircraft, but later I heard that all the pilots that had ditched in the sea were rescued by the rescue submarine or other warships in the area. When we went in we could see that there were more aircraft on the ground and these were strafed and destroyed while the Avengers bombed the runways, putting them out of action.'

Attacks were also made on various small craft on the water and a number of lorry loads of Japanese troops were strafed. Some aircraft were stored in cave shelters and they were bombed by SAP (Semi-Armoured Piercing) bombs.

One Corsair pilot from 1836 Squadron on HMS *Victorious* had been part of the escort for the Avengers bombing strikes. After seeing them in, he was involved in strafing the barges on the water, which were set on fire. Just then another Corsair pilot reported to him that he had smoke coming out of his aircraft. On checking the oil gauge he saw that it was at zero and knowing that the engine would soon seize up, flew out about a mile from the island and ditched in the sea. The Corsair stayed afloat long enough for the pilot to get out and into his dinghy, while one of the other pilots stayed overhead and radioed his position to the fleet. After two hours, it was getting dark and he saw a craft in the distance, which eventually turned out to be the American rescue submarine USS *Bluefish*. After he was safely picked up, he met on board the submarine an Avenger crew from HMS *Indomitable* who had been rescued after ditching, as well as another American airman who had been rescued.

Each day the radar surveillance and destroyers were stationed away from the Task Force to identify any kamikaze attack threats to the fleet. However, on the 17th May there were mechanical problems with HMS *Indomitable* which affected her speed and safe operation of aircraft, followed by a Corsair crash landing on HMS *Victorious* and going straight through the crash barriers killing three, including the pilot, and injuring four. Later, another aircraft bounced between the barriers, damaging Corsairs and Avengers. Aircraft from HMS *Victorious* were then directed to land on other carriers.

The decision was made not to undertake the remaining three strikes planned for that day. With the only strike that took place, all runways on Ishigaki airfields were cratered and put out of action, but there was doubt that the position was similar on the Miyako airfields. TF 57 then left for refuelling and replenishment of supplies, aircraft and ammunition, in Area Cootie, while the American Task Group 52.1.3 was tasked again to take over.

On the 18th May at Area Cootie, TF 57 started the refuelling and replenishment, but at 11.03 hours there was a hanger fire in HMS *Formidable* caused by a Corsair's guns being accidently fired and hitting an Avenger, which then exploded causing the fire. The fire was difficult to extinguish, and the water drenching that was implemented caused 7 Avengers and 21 Corsairs to be damaged, their condition described as 'varying from complete loss to flyable duds'. Arrangements were then made to fly in replaceable aircraft from the escort carrier HMS *Ruler*, and for the 'flyable duds' to be flown to escort carrier HMS *Chaser* which was on ferry duties taking aircraft away for repair. The hospital ship *Tjitjalengka* was contacted by aircraft while in its waiting area, and came in to take on board the sick and the wounded from HMS *Formidable*.

On the 20th May the fleet returned to its flying off area, but ran into fog at 05.15 hours, and the destroyer HMS *Quilliam,* while manoeuvring at the stern of HMS *Indomitable*, collided and seriously damaged its bow. The destroyer had more severe damage than the carrier and was taken in tow by HMAS *Norman*, while HMS *Black Prince* was tasked to escort the tow to Area Cootie. This was a difficult tow, because due to the cable being attached to the stern of HMS *Quilliam*, the damaged bow was dragging in the water and made it very difficult for HMAS *Norman* to tow. HMS *Black Prince* took over and also found the tow difficult, but once at Area Cootie the tug *Weasel* was to take over the tow, with HMS *Ruler* providing the air cover. Fortunately, there were no casualties in this incident.

Sub. Lt. Wright and his TAG crew had taken off in JZ624 from HMS Indomitable for their intended strike on Ishigaki airfield:

'We found the weather was 10/10 overcast and it was impossible to launch a strike, so we had to return to the carrier and land on deck, still with our bombs on board. We made up for it the next day, when we took off, again in TBM JZ624, for two attacks on Ishigaki airfield. The first attack on the airfield was at 08.55 when we made a successful strike on the E-W runway of Ishigaki airfield.

The second attack was again in JZ624 at 14.40, but when we arrived over the intended target on Ishigaki, the weather had deteriorated, with the airfield were covered by low cloud. Rather than return with our bombs again, we could see buildings on the hill tops that were appropriate targets, so we bombed those instead.'

Attack on Ishigaki airfield.   *Courtesy of Paul Whiteing*

As well as the two strikes on Ishigaki, there were three on Miyako, and these took place at 6.55, 12.10 and 16.10, when both Hirara and Nobara were cratered and put out of action. Strikes also took place on the warehouse area in Hirara town and other installations, including a tented camp used by Japanese troops, and this was also strafed. A close watch was maintained for enemy aircraft and one identified as a Myrt was shot down by Hellcats from HMS *Indomitable*, and this was the last Japanese aircraft to be shot down by Task Force 57 during the Operation Iceberg campaign.

That day a message was received from the Commander of the Fifth Fleet indicating the future deployment of the British Pacific Fleet, and the decision was made to release HMS *Formidable* early to sail to Sydney for repairs, so that the Task Force would have four carriers available for the next deployment with the US Fleet. The Task Force detached from the flying off positions and left for refuelling and replenishment at Area Cootie, while the US Task Unit 52.1.3 took over.

Rear Admiral's TU 52.1.3 carriers, including USS *Suwannee, Santee, Chenago* and *Block Island II*, took over again on the 23rd May with the resumption of strikes on Ishigaki and Miyako. Although poor visibility and rain on Miyako reduced the number of strikes that could be undertaken, the day's tally included damage to the runways, surrounding buildings, aircraft destroyed on the ground and strikes on coastal vessels.

On arrival at Area Cootie in the early morning of the 22nd May, refuelling and replenishment commenced. HMS *Quilliam*, towed by the tug *Weasel* and escorted by HMS *Black Prince*, HMS *Grenville*, HMAS *Norman* and HMS *Ruler* had also arrived. After various organisational arrangements had been dealt with, the tug *Weasel* then left, towing HMS *Quilliam*, with HMAS *Norman* as escort. However, because of the difficulty the tug *Weasel* was having towing the destroyer, a request was made for a more powerful tug, and the American tug *Turkey* was sent to take over the tow to Leyte. HMS *Formidable,* due to the battle damage it had received, also left later that day for Manus, for temporary repairs before proceeding to Sydney. The carrier was escorted by HMS *Kempenfelt* and HMS *Whirlwind*, which were also due for refits.

On May 22nd Sub. Lt. Wright had quite an interesting day:

'I was tasked to fly replacement aircraft back to HMS *Indomitable* and was taken aboard by the destroyer HMS *Undaunted* and transferred by Breeches Buoy to the escort carrier HMS *Speaker*. Once on board I was directed to Avenger FN915 and took off by means of an accelerated take off and flew the aircraft to HMS *Indomitable.'*

The next day the replenishment of fuel and stores continued, but during the day two Hellcats from HMS *Chaser* crashed into the sea with the loss of both pilots. The Task Force left at 18.15 hours with just three carriers, to return to the flying off area and recommence operations on the Sakishima Gunto. Due to the reduction of one carrier the five strikes per day were reduced to four, with the first strike not starting so early in the morning.

Pilot transferring by Breeches Buoy. Courtesy of Paul Whiteing

The strike on the 24th May for Sub. Lt. Wright and his crew, Sub. Lt. Studd and P.O. Scougall, was quite disappointing. Early in the morning the weather was overcast and raining, and flying was delayed until aircraft observing the weather sent back reports that the weather was improving, therefore the first strikes for Miyako took off later in the morning:

> 'I took off with my crew, Sub. Lt. Studd and P.O. Scougall, for a strike on Miyako at 10.45 hours. When we arrived over the target we went into a dive attack, but we didn't hit anything in particular and came home quite disappointed.'

Hirara and Nobara airfields were in fact hit and cratered, and again put out of action. The strikes on Ishigaki airfield put all the runways out of action, with no indication of Japanese air activity and no losses to the Task Force.

May 25th was the last day of combat operations for Operation Iceberg, and due to an early morning clearing sky, the first of three strikes was able to take off at 06.00 hours, with strikes on Miyako and Ishigaki. Sub. Lt. Wright and his crew were to undertake their final strikes in Sakishima Gunto:

> 'I took off with my TAG crew in JZ624 for our final strikes
> on Ishigaki and Miyako airfields. We bombed the runways
> of Ishigaki and Miyara airfields, and also made a strike on
> the intersection of Hirara airfield, Miyako. There was
> nothing much to report and we didn't see any enemy aircraft.
> It looked as though we had succeeded in our mission.'

HMS *Indomitable*, with the remaining carriers, left the operational
area on May 25th to sail for Manus and then to Sydney, having
completed her operational duties with Task Force 57. Later that
day, HMS *King George V* and destroyers, HMS *Troubridge,* HMS
Tenacious and HMS *Termagant*, sailed to Guam, arriving on the
28th May. On the 29th May, Admiral Nimitz boarded HMS *King
George V* and was entertained by the Vice Admiral Rawlings,
Second in Command of the British Pacific Fleet.

Rear Admiral Sample's TU52.1.3 took over the strikes on the
islands from 26th to 28th May, but on the 28th May the US Third
Fleet, commanded by Admiral Halsey, were to take over from the
Fifth Fleet. Task Force 58 then became Task Force 38, and Rear
Admiral Sample's Task Units 52.1.3 were re-designated to 32.1.3,
with the strikes on Sakishima Gunto continuing from the 30th May
through to the 24th June, with the eventual surrender of the
Ryukyu Islands being signed by General Noumi on the 7th
September, 1945.

The British Pacific Fleet leave for Sydney, Australia

The remainder of Task Force 57 refuelled at Area Cootie, before
sailing for Manus where they arrived on the 30th May. The ships
left again on the 31st May for Sydney, and while at sea, Sub. Lt.
Wright's log book reveals that on the 1st June he took off with PO
Hodgson in Avenger TBM JZ624, to take part in a '4-carrier
rendezvous and break-up-drill'. The ships of the Task Force
arrived at Sydney on the 5th June, when the tasks of replenishment,
repairs and servicing the vessels took place, in advance of the fleet
sailing again to prepare for 'Operation Olympic', the invasion of
Japan. While in Sydney, the crews had the opportunity of shore
leave before embarking again on their next mission.

CHAPTER 21

British Pacific Fleet Task Force 57, Sydney, Australia

After arrival in Sydney on the 5th June 1945, 857 Squadron Avengers and 1839 and 1844 Squadron Hellcats were due to fly off HMS *Indomitable* for RNAS Nowra, which was about 77miles (125km) from Sydney, where the squadron was to be billeted. When Sub. Lt. Wright, with PO Scougall, took off on the 6th June to fly to the RNAS Nowra, he refers to being 'squirted off', which is the pilot's term for being catapulted off from the carrier's flight deck. The next day, 849 Squadron Avengers left HMS *Victorious* for RNAS Nowra.

As 857 Squadron would not be taking part in the next mission, the aircrews still had to maintain practice manoeuvres and Sub. Lt. Wright refers to the constant practice they did while based at RNAS Nowra throughout June and July, while HMS *Indomitable* was being refitted in Sydney:

'The squadron was kept busy all the time so that we didn't get bored, so we returned to practising manoeuvres. This included a range of practice manoeuvres, including touch and go on the airfield, turret air to sea firing, glide bombing practice, night flying, night ADDLs and local flying with two landings, low flying, pilot navigation over sea, tail chasing and cross country flights.'

Sub. Lt. Wright's crew members during this time included Sub. Lt. Glendinning, PO Hodgson, PO Scougall, PO With, PO Pettit, PO Ellis, L/A Fox, PO Spetch, AM Welwyns, AML Elliott and L/A Fox.

Operation Inmate interlude

HMS *Implacable* had arrived at Manus on the 29th May 1945, to begin a six week work up period, and undertook flying exercises off Manus during the 11th to 12th June 1945, before joining Task Group 111.2.

'Operation Inmate' was an attack on the Truk Atoll, Caroline Islands, by the British Pacific Fleet as 'TG 111.2' under the command of Rear-Admiral Brind, on the 14th to 15th June 1945.

TG 11.2 included:

Carrier, HMS *Implacable*:

        801 Squadron (Lt. Cdr. Jewers) Seafires,

        828 Squadron (Lt. Cdr. Swanton) Avengers,

        880 Squadron (Lt. Cdr. Crosley) Seafires,

        and 1771 Squadron (Lt. Cdr. MacWhirter) Fireflies,

Escort carrier, HMS *Ruler*,

Cruisers, HMS *Swiftsure*, HMS *Newfoundland*, RCN *Uganda*
      and RMZN *Achilles*,

Covered by the destroyers, HMS *Troubridge*, HMS *Teazer*,
      HMS *Tenacious*, HMS *Termagant* and HMS *Terpsichore*.

HMS *Implacable* and the other cruisers and destroyers were newly arrived, and the aim of Operation Inmate was to give this Task Group an opportunity to get some experience in combat operations in the Pacific theatre. The American fleet had already given the Truk Atoll some attention over the past year and it was the aim of this attack to take out its airfields and aircraft to ensure that they could not attack and damage the ships and aircraft of the British Pacific Fleet in its future combat action in the Pacific.

On the 10th June, HMS *Implacable* sailed from Manus for the attack on the Truck Atoll, code named Operation Inmate. At dawn on the 14th June 1945, HMS *Implacable* launched a Ramrod by four Fireflies and 12 Seafires, followed later by CAP (Combat Air Patrol). The 'Ramrod' was a fighter sweep against ground targets that included a radar station and an airfield, but one of 801 Squadron Seafires was hit by flak over the airfield and crashed with the loss of the pilot. However, not only were the Seafires useful for Ramrod attacks and CAPs, but could be used for Photo Reconnaissance, and one of the Seafire FIII carried a camera and was able to bring back photographs of airfields, other military installations and coastal defences, which were essential for planning the following attacks. Further attacks continued for the remainder of the day, causing more damage to the Japanese airfields and defences. As the aircraft returned to HMS *Implacable* after all sorties had been completed and the deck landings were completed successfully, although there was always HMS *Ruler* available as a spare deck for any emergency landings, or for refuelling and rearming. HMS *Ruler* also had on board a Supermarine amphibious Walrus for Air Sea Rescue, from 1701 Squadron, but a severe storm blew up and the aircraft was blown over the side and lost in the sea.

On the 15th June there was more of a concentration on bombardment from the ships, and although some enemy aircraft had been spotted, the CAP was covered by 12 Seafires, where 6 covered the carriers and 6 covered the ships. There was some night flying conducted by Avengers from 828 Squadron, but once they had landed back on board, the Task Group left the area to return to Manus.

Although the Seafires took part in Ramrod attacks on ground targets, they were also used for CAP (Combat Air Patrols) and Jack Patrols. When on the 'Jack Patrols' the flight consisted of 8 Seafires, each carrying extra fuel in 90 gallon slipper tanks to allow for a more extended time in the air while maintaining CAP.

Jack patrols were introduced by the Americans in an attempt to deal with kamikaze aircraft that may have avoided aircraft patrolling further out, or may be coming in at low level and dangerously close to attacking the fleet. Jack Patrols are groups of fighters patrolling at approximately 10 miles from the fleet and flying at an altitude of 3,000 feet (900 meters) while covering the four points of the compass, North, South, East and West. The Seafire LF III was to prove itself the best aircraft for its interceptor role, with its fast acceleration and rate of climb it could attack targets identified by radar at any altitude in the shortest time. The attacking Seafire, with its two 20mm Hispano cannons and four 0.303 Browning machine guns, was deadly against the Japanese Zeke (Zero), which was not armoured or protected with self-sealing fuel tanks. Once the Seafire had fired its cannons and machine guns and hit a Zero, because of the Zero's lack of armour the fuselage would be smashed to pieces, with its fuel igniting, causing the aircraft to explode and go down in flames.

The kamikaze suicide attacks were causing serious problems with the American carriers, which had wooden flight decks, but despite the armoured decks of the British carriers, which could get a carrier back in action in a fairly short time, damage was still inflicted upon aircraft and personnel on the flight decks. It was essential for the air patrols, including the Jack Patrols, to detect and attack these suicide aircraft before they dived on the aircraft carriers or warships. Although being subject to the last screen of intercepting aircraft, there was always kamikaze aircraft that managed to get through, however many were shot down before they could initiate their suicide dive.

The Battle for Okinawa ends

The battle for Okinawa came to an end on the 22nd June, and the full extent of American losses to its ships through kamikaze attacks amounted to over 5,000 men, with many of their carriers that had not been sunk, spending many months in dock being repaired before returning to active service.

It was also on the 22nd June that Sub. Lt. Wright went solo in a Hellcat from RNAS Nowra, for a familiarization flight and did a stall, loop, slow roll and landing.

Having learned to fly in the N.P.1, N.2.S, SNV and SNJ, before the TBF Avenger, Sub. Lt. Wright had never had the opportunity to fly the Tiger Moth, which was the first aircraft that many pilots had their first experience of flying:

'It was interesting that I had learned to fly in the USA, but had not experienced flying a Tiger Moth, which many trainee pilots have their first flights in. I was ordered by the Commander (Flying) that in accordance with requirements I was to receive cockpit instruction and be examined on my flying of the Tiger Moth. On the 28th June 1945, with Sub. Lt. Foster as pilot and me as passenger, I went up in Tiger Moth A17 497 for familiarization, where we practised 3 touch-and-go, 2 stalls and landings. Later that day I went up again, but this time as pilot with my regular navigator, Sub. Lt. Glendinning, for local flying, 2 stalls, 2 spins, 1 loop and steep turns. I was passed out as satisfactory.'

Construction number DHA920 Type DH82A Tiger Moth was listed as with the RAAF as A17-497, but crashed in August 1944 and was 'reduced to spares'. However, Sub. Lt. Wright flew Tiger Moth A17-497 on the 28th June 1945, so the aircraft appears to have later been restored to flying.

Task Force 37 leaves Sydney for Operation Olympic

849 Squadron Avengers left RNAS Nowra on the 24th June to re-embark on HMS *Victorious* in advance of the ships of the British Pacific Fleet, which had been re-designated 'Task Force 37', leaving Sydney on the 28th June with new air crews to join the US Task Force 38 for 'Operation Olympic', as part of 'Operation Downfall', the planned invasion of Japan.

The British Pacific Fleet Task Force 37 consisted of:

HMS *King George V* (Flag Admiral Rawlings)

with the Fleet carriers:

HMS *Implacable*: 48 Seafires, 12 Firefly, 18 Avengers
HMS *Formidable*: 6 Hellcats, 36 Corsairs, 12 Avengers
HMS *Victorious*: 37 Corsairs,14 Avengers, 2 Walrus

accompanied by the cruisers: HMS *Newfoundland*,
HMS *Black Prince*,   RNZN *Achilles,*
RNZN *Gambia,*   RCN *Uganda*

and the destroyers: HMS *Grenville*,
HMS *Ulysses*,   HMS *Undaunted*,
HMS *Undine*,   HMS *Urania,*
HMS *Urchin*,   HMS *Troubridge*,
HMS *Teazer*,   HMS *Tenacious*,
HMS *Termagant*,   HMS *Terpsichore*,
HMS *Quadrant*,   HMS *Quality*,
RAN *Quieron*   RAN *Quickmatch.*

NB. HMS *Indefatigable* (48 Seafires, 12 Firefly, 18 Avengers) was unable to sail with the fleet due to having defective equipment.

HMS *Indomitable* did not sail with the Task Force 37 and was relieved by HMS *Implacable* while she was refitted in Sydney. After refitting was completed, HMS *Indomitable* remained in Sydney throughout July. Due to HMS *Indomitable* not sailing with Task Force 37, Admiral Vain's flag was transferred to HMS *Formidable.*

Task Force 37 reached Manus and from the 4th to 6th July undertook replenishment. Just after the Fleet left Manus, HMS *Implacable* had problems with one of her propeller shaft bearings and had to undertake repairs. Further refuelling was done at sea on the 13th July, and a first was when HMS *King George V* was able to refuel alongside a tanker, a procedure which was later to be established as the norm.

Both the British Task Force 37 and the US Task Force 38 of the US Navy Third Fleet joined together on the 16th July to attack targets on the Japanese mainland, including attacks on airfields and railways. The first strikes started on the 17th to 19th July, with the aircraft from HMS *Formidable* and HMS *Implacable* being the first British aircraft to strike mainland Japan. Some strikes were called off because of bad weather conditions due to it being the Typhoon season in the area.

Two of the aims of Admiral Halsey were to destroy the remaining Imperial Japanese Navy anchored in the Inland Sea around Kure, and to challenge the Japanese aircraft which undoubtedly would be searching for the American Task Force 38 and British Task Force 37. The American and British Task Forces conducted massive air strikes in the Inland Sea and the area around Kure, and this included the Kure naval base where many of the Imperial Japanese Navy ships were gathered. They succeeded in sinking the aircraft carrier *Amagi*, battleships *Hyuga*, *Haruna* and *Ise*, cruisers, *Tone*, *Aoba*, *Oyodo*, and training cruisers *Iwate* and *Izumo*, along with a large number of warships damaged. The Americans got their revenge for the Japanese attack on Pearl Harbour, when they attacked the Yokosuka naval base, the largest base in Japan, on the 18th July.

Task Force 37 left for refuelling and replenishment on the 19th July, which took place from the 20th to 22nd July, and included

HMS *Indefatigable* which had arrived from Manus. The weather was so bad at that time that it increased the time taken for replenishment while at sea, but the British fleet still sank two escort ships and attacked and badly damaged the *Kaiyo*, an IJN escort carrier which had previously hit a mine. It had been attacked by US bombers during July, and by 10th August was listing so badly, with her flight deck under water, that her captain ordered the crew ashore.

In addition to the aircraft strikes, well targeted naval bombardments took place during July and August and did a lot of damage to the industrial production in Japan. This also impacted upon the morale of the workers, which then reflected upon decreased production. The bombing of Japanese civilian and military areas, including airfields and dockyards started in the southeast and moved gradually up the coast, causing increasing destruction to the Japanese infrastructure.

Japan accepts the terms of the Potsdam Declaration

The attacks continued into August, but despite all the attacks on the cities, industrial and production sites, such as airfields and dockyards, that were destroyed by the bombing, the Japanese government and military still did not give in. It was finally left to the US Air Force B-29 Superfortress *Enola Gay* dropping the first atomic bomb on Hiroshima on the 6th August 1945, followed by a second atomic bomb dropped on Nagasaki on the 9th August 1945, to force the Japanese to the negotiating table.

Despite meetings with Japanese negotiators for surrender terms, the fighting still went on and the Allies returned to further attacks on the Japanese mainland. These attacks were fiercely defended by the Japanese aircraft, many of which were shot down or destroyed on the ground. It appeared that the Japanese intended fight to the end to die with honour, but it was Emperor Hirohito that made the final decision to surrender to the allies, against the wishes of many of his military generals and politicians. This he did by recording a message on the 14th August, for broadcast at noon on the 15th August 1945.

By this time the majority of the British Pacific Fleet had already left mainland Japan for Manus, then arriving back at Sydney from the 23rd August, leaving the flagship HMS *King George V* and HMS *Indefatigable* behind to attend the formal surrender. The formal surrender was taken by General MacArthur on board the US battleship USS *Missouri* on the morning of the 2nd September 1945, when General Umezu of the Japanese Imperial General Staff signed the surrender documents.

Over 4,000 Japanese pilots had taken part in kamikaze attacks, and at the surrender of Japan to the allies in August 1945, Vice-Admiral Onishi, who instigated the kamikaze attacks, committed ritual suicide. He left a message apologising to all the kamikaze suicide pilots that were killed, and promoted that Japan embarked on creating a future of living in peace with other countries.

CHAPTER 22

857 Squadron in
Australia and Hong Kong July-October 1945

July 1945

Sub. Lt. Wright continued further practice manoeuvres from their base at RN Air Station, Nowra. On his first flight in TBM JZ629 with his crew, A/M Goldsmith, A/M Rainbow, he took for a radio test flight and then with PO Middleton, practised wingovers and low flying. On the 20th July, Sub. Lt. Wright undertook a formation cross country flight from Nowra to Canberra in JZ373 and return, practicing low level flying. Then it was a resumption to practice for a return to HMS *Indomitable*. This included plenty of ADDLs, and although Sub. Lt. Wright had practiced night ADDLs during June and July, it was on the 26th July that he took part in JZ441 for night deck landings on HMS *Indomitable*, after which he flew back to RNAS Nowra.

August 1945

On the 1st August Sub. Lt. Wright was taken as passenger to RNAS Bankstown, Sydney, (MONAB 2) and flew JZ394 back to RNAS Nowra (MONAB 1). The next day he flew JZ627 from RNAS Nowra to rejoin HMS *Indomitable*. Both 1839 and 1844 Corsairs left RNAS Nowra on the 3rd August to rejoin HMS *Indomitable*.

Further practice manoeuvres took place with his crew, Sub. Lt. Buckle and P.O. Aston, for take-off trials with 4 x 500lb bombs. This resulted in a satisfactory take-off with 25 knot wind and a 570ft run. The next day, August 6th, there was catapult practice, where Sub. Lt. Wright, with P.O. Scougall, was to be 'squirted off', but the catapult strop broke and in his words, 'take-off was difficult!' However, the 10th August really stuck in his memory when he did a practice strike on two airfields at dusk with P.O. Scougall:

'On the 10th August, when practising night flying as a

prelude to becoming a night nuisance raider over Japan, I was preparing to make a deck landing and was under the control of the aircraft carrier, who said, 'We will accept you, if we can,' because they were dealing with a crashed aircraft on the flight deck. I received a red flare to go around again, but when I came around again I was committed to landing and under the direction of the batsman. Some idiot sent up a powerful white flare and I was blinded, but still under the batsman's control, and thought I would be alright. The aircraft was slipping to the right and crashed into the carrier's island on landing, damaging the starboard wing, propeller and engine. The aircraft was a write-off and so they pushed the wreck over the side.

The reason for the accident was given as pilot error and no action was taken, but the truth was one of the carrier crew accidently let off a flare just as I was landing. It destroyed my night vision and this was what caused the accident.

The next day I was back to flying a Balbo over Sydney with 6 Avengers from 857 Squadron and 16 Hellcats from 1844 Squadron in close formation. My crew for that flight was PO Scougall, PO Ellison and PO Spetch.'

A 'Balbo' was a term used in the 1930-40s to describe a large formation of aircraft, and was used during the Battle of Britain for the Duxford Big Wings. It originates from an Italian ace, Italo Balbo, who used large aircraft formations in the 1930s to promote Italian aviation.

Task Group 111.2 sail for the British re-occupation of Hong Kong

In advance of the surrender of Japan, Task Groups had been prepared for the regaining of Hong Kong (TG111.2), Shanghai (TG111.3), and Singapore (TG 111.4), from Japanese occupation. Within two hours of the acceptance of the terms of surrender of Japan by Emperor Hirohito on the 15th August 1945, the Task Groups had sailed from Sydney.

That same day, Sub. Lt. Wright and Sub. Lt. Smith took off to ferry a plane from RNAS Bankstown to HMS *Indomitable*, before the Task Group left for Hong Kong.

HMS *Indomitable* (Flag Admiral Harcourt Commanding 11 Aircraft Squadron) sailed from Sydney as part of Task Group 111.2 to re-occupy Hong Kong. Admiral Harcourt was to become Commander in Chief, Hong Kong. It had been a speedy departure because of rumours that the Americans had hoped to reach Hong Kong before the British, and the British government wanted the British Pacific Fleet to take the surrender of ports in the old British Empire. The Task Group consisted of HMS *Venerable*, a light fleet carrier, HMS *Swiftsure*, HMS *Black Prince*, HHS *Euryalus*, HMCS *Prince Robert* cruisers, and the destroyers HMS *Kempenfelt*, HMS *Ursa*, HMS *Quadrant* and HMS *Whirlwind*.

While at sea, practice manoeuvres still continued and on the 23rd August Sub. Lt. Wright remembers taking part in a Balbo over Leyte, with two dummy attacks on a ship. Five days later, Sub. Lt. Wright, with Sub. Lt. Glendinning and P.O. Scougall, undertook gunnery practice with front and turret guns, which was to become very important when they arrived in Hong Kong harbour. They had been warned of an EMB (Explosive Motor Boat) base on Lamma Island, where it was believed there were some 'kamikaze caves' where the boats were kept. These belonged to the 'Special Attack Shinyo Squadron'.

When the Task Group reached Hong Kong, they were joined by the battleship HMS *Anson* and aircraft carrier HMS *Vengeance*, before entry to Hong Kong following the completion of minesweeping. On the 30th August, Avengers took off to patrol over Hong Kong with 4 x 500lb bombs covering the Fleet's entry into Victoria Harbour. Sub. Lt. Wright, with P.O. Scougall in TBM JZ131, succeeded with the other Avengers in destroying a number of the Japanese EMB suicide boats carrying explosives, thus ensuring the safe entry to Hong Kong:

'That strike was needed because a patrol had spotted some six Japanese Motor Boats approaching our ship at high speed, in spite of warnings that no shipping movements would be tolerated. We on board HMS *Indomitable* were told to get airborne immediately, as six Jap suicide boats all carrying white flags were coming towards us. All twelve Avengers took off, but we had to jettison our bombs on take-off, because of a ropey engine. We carried on with machine guns right into attack formation and went straight in and sunk the lot.'

Admiral Harcourt and a party of officers went ashore to set up their base in the Peninsular Hotel, Hong Kong; this was the very hotel where the British surrendered to the Japanese in December 1941. During the war, the hotel remained the administrative centre for the Japanese, but in September 1945 the Japanese officially surrendered Hong Kong back to the British at the Governor's residence.

Hong Kong 1945.   *Frank Stockwell*

In Hong Kong

Although V-J Day was declared on the 15th August 1945, there were still a threat of attacks by Japanese troops in Hong Kong, as proved by the suicide boats on the 30th August while entering Hong Kong waters, and it appeared that the Japanese troops either did not know about the surrender or were not taking any notice. The decision was to have armed patrols, and officers carried their pistols to deal with any enemy resistance. Sub. Lt. Wright was posted ashore to take charge of transport, and was based in a very comfortable hotel, which he found very relaxing and also had some good fun.

His job was not easy, and for someone in charge of transport, he had difficulty in finding transport to get around himself:

'At the time we were the first ship to disembark naval personnel. I managed to acquire a motorcycle by various means, but by then other ships had docked and more sailors were around. This was when I lost my motorbike to three sailors from a destroyer, who pinched it and took it on board their ship.

There I was again without transport, but down the road towards me came a beautiful British sports car. I took out my pistol and put up my hand to stop the driver. He stopped and got out of the car. I told him that I was commandeering the car and if he did not hand it over in five seconds I would shoot. Amazingly, he spoke perfect English and promptly agreed to let me have the car. I was able to use the car for the two weeks we were in Hong Kong.'

Hong Kong waterfront.   *Geoffrey Wright*

Japanese troops surrendering in Hong Kong.   Geoffrey Wright Collection

HMS Indomitable at anchor.   Geoffrey Wright Collection

'We found that some of the Japanese soldiers didn't know that the war had ended and there were some quite difficult

212

moments. One being the twenty Japanese soldiers occupying the San Miguel Brewery, but we did have a translator who was able to solve that problem. It is believed that the Royal Marines who took over the brewery went missing for about two hours. This caused some worry, but when a very tipsy group of marines were eventually found, it was clear they had been busy tasting the local brew.'

Japanese negotiator on HMS Indomitable.   Geoffrey Wright Collection

The actual Japanese negotiations for surrender took place initially on HMS *Indomitable* when a Japanese negotiator was flown in carrying a packet in his hand. After discussing with British naval officers the details of the surrender, he was escorted by Royal Marines along the flight deck and returned in the aircraft, which then took off with him to prepare for the actual surrender.

'I witnessed the surrender at Government House with Admiral Sir Bruce Fraser and Admiral Harcourt, the Hong Kong Commander in Chief, as the British officers and Rear Admiral Ruitaro Fujita for the Japanese. Captain Eccles, our captain on HMS *Indomitable*, was a fluent Japanese speaker and acted as the interpreter. The Japanese did not appear very happy, although they did salute. Once the British soldiers arrived we handed over Hong Kong and sailed for Sydney shortly after.'

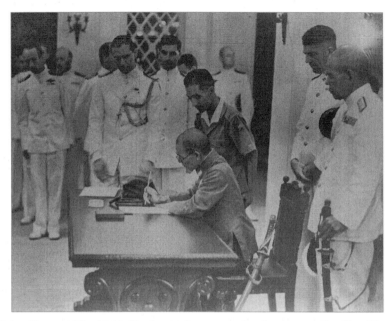

Major General Umekichi Okada signing surrender document. Geoffrey Wright

Rear Admiral Ruitaro Fujita signing the surrender document.   Geoffrey Wright

After returning to Sydney there was not much flying for Sub. Lt. Wright, but on the 28th September he took part in some flight drill with P.O. Scougall in JZ448. On the 3rd October, Sub. Lt. Wright flew JZ131 from HMS *Indomitable* to RNAS Bankstown. In his logbook he writes, 'From *Indomitable* to Bankstown to get rid of the squadron planes.'

On the 4th October, the remaining aircraft from HMS *Indomitable* flew in formation over the city as a last farewell, and Sub. Lt. Wright had quite an experience, which could have been fateful in its outcome.

'My last flight in an Avenger was on the 4th October 1945, which was, I believe, the last landing I ever carried out on HMS *Indomitable*. The landing was so awful the Batsman threw his bats into the sea in disgust.

I was the last plane to take off, but with great difficulty, because the plane felt excessively tail heavy. On returning to the carrier I was again last to land and made such a heavy landing I thought the plane would collapse, but it didn't – more luck than judgement!

The deck landing officer (I think it was Joe Brough) rushed up the deck and shouted, 'Wilbur, that was the most bloody awful landing I've ever seen.' With that he walked to the edge of the flight deck and threw his two bats into the sea.

I soon discovered the reason for my worse than usual flying. There is a small door in the side of the Avenger, quite a long way aft, which gives access to the Telegraphist/Air Gunner's radio cabin, and from there to the rotating gun turret where he normally sits during flights. After I had landed, the door flew open and six or seven sailors emerged at high speed, and disappeared below deck before I had recovered from the shock.

As it was our last flight from HMS *Indomitable* I thought it prudent not to pursue the matter, but I have often wondered since if the stowaways ever realised how nearly it was literally the last flight for all of us in the plane that day.'

Sub. Lt. Wright took-off again in JZ441 for his final flight back to RNAS Bankstown, and this was to be his final flight in the Pacific. His logbook final entry from active service was '557.35 hours'.

Post-Pacific War

The British Pacific Fleet stayed in the Far East after the surrender and helped with repatriation of prisoners of war, including supplying desperately needed first aid and food to the people in the region. But later, without much recognition for what it had achieved in the Pacific war, the British Pacific Fleet was largely 'The Forgotten Fleet.'

'Farewell Sydney!' HMS Indomitable leaving Sydney
to return to Portsmouth, England.
Courtesy of Paul Whiteing

HMS *Indomitable* remained with the British Pacific Fleet until November and returned to the UK in December 1945. Sub. Lt. Wright remembers the return to the United Kingdom well:

'I returned to Portsmouth in HMS *Indomitable* and into the docks flying the 100ft pennant, but there appeared to be very little fuss or celebration for our return from the war in the Pacific. We were sent on leave very quickly, because we were all due for promotion, but this was shortly followed by a letter and £300 gratuity, so we were all demobbed.'

After being demobbed from the Fleet Air Arm, Geoffrey Eaton Wright returned to Cambridge to finish his BA in Law, and then an MA. His father had been to Cambridge, but went on to complete his PhD and suggested that his son did so as well, but Geoffrey Wright did not want to do that and became a solicitor, eventually having his own practice.

EPILOGUE

Post War Flying

Flying again in the Royal Air Force Volunteer Reserve after the War

Geoffrey Eaton Wright had not considered flying again after the war, and yet flying was still in his blood:

'I was not keen to fly again, but after a short while I changed my mind and went to Fairoaks on October 16th 1948 for a flying test in a Tiger Moth. I remember flying the Tiger Moth while with 857 Squadron in Australia on the 28th June 1945. That was when Sub. Lt. Foster took me up for a familiarization, and then the same day I went solo, practicing manoeuvres and flying around the local area.

As part of my RAFVR, from December 4th 1948, through to July 12th 1949, I was training with No 18 Reserve Flying School at Fairoaks, starting my 15 days reserve training from 18th June 1949. On August 12th I had already completed a checkflight with an instructor in an Auster G-AHSO, and followed this up later that day with taking my wife up in the aircraft for a local flight.

It was not until the 4th February 1950, that I again flew again, and this continued a few days a month, and increasing in July, counting the annual 15 days reserve training days of flying for No 18 Reserve Flying School, from 8th July 1950 flying the Tiger Moth and Chipmunk. I also did some time in the simulator, but that was mainly for navigation training.'

From the 9th August to September 13th 1951, Fl. Lt. Wright trained with No 22 FTS (Flying Training School) at RAF Syerston, nr Newark, Nottinghamshire, flying the North American Harvard. The No 6 course ended on the 13th September 1951. By this time his flying hours were 681hrs 40mins.

RAF Full Sutton was re-opened in 1951 as a result of the

Korean War emergency. Its aim was to act as a RFS (Refresher Flying School) for the RAFVR (Royal Air Force Volunteer Reserve). RFS remained at Full Sutton until 1955 when it became a reserve site for two years for the US Air Force, due to the Cold War. In the event, it was not used operationally by the US Air Force.

The aircraft being flown at RAF Full Sutton from 1951, was the Spitfire XVI which had the Packard Merlin 266 engine. The aircraft was built specifically for low level work, and originally built with clipped wings for ease of roll.

Two of the Spitfire Mk XVIs which were involved in the RFS training at RAF Full Sutton were SM411, which transferred in June 1951 to No 103 FRS, and TB572 that also went to 103 FRS.

Fl. Lt. Wright remembers his time at Full Sutton very clearly:

'From September 25th 1951, I transferred to No 1 Squadron Unit 103 RAF Full Sutton to November 1951, when I flew Spitfire XVIs, Vampire Is and Meteor VII jets, as it was thought (wrongly as it turned out), that we would be needed in the Korean War. In 1952 I was with 207 A.F.S. (Advanced Flying School) Full Sutton, and then in 1953 with 203 AFS Driffield, Yorkshire, flying Meteors during my annual 15 days training, but then the RAFVR was disbanded. I had my last flight in a Meteor IV VZ419 when I practiced aerobatics. In February 1966 I went on my first and only flight in a helicopter, a Colt G-ARSV at Hurn airport, Bournemouth.

My total flying hours at the end of my flying career was 748hr 20mins, since then I have only done a little gliding from time to time, but even that not recently. My rank from being commissioned in January 1944 was Sub Lieutenant in the Navy, but a Flight Lieutenant in the Royal Air Force.

Finally, I would like to testify to the thoroughness and efficiency of the training I received during the war from the United States Navy. The Americans were very good in allowing you to fly any of their planes. If you asked, the answer was usually 'sure'.

The aircraft were always first class and the instructors all the way through my training were excellent. The Avenger was an extremely rugged plane, well suited to its task. Although it flew like a lump of lead, it was an excellent carrier borne plane. The excellence of training continued during the post-war period and I feel privileged to have had the opportunity of adding that to my flying experience.'

Geoffrey Eaton Wright's final words were of the sadness he felt for the loss of so many of his colleagues:

'The greatest sadness I have is that I lost a lot of my colleagues, who had bailed out of their aircraft, or had crashed and survived, only to be captured by the Japanese. It was well known by us that if we were captured by the Japanese we would be first tortured and then beheaded by an officer with a Samurai sword. I have also heard that some Fleet Air Arm pilots were even executed after the Japanese had surrendered in 1945.

When I heard, 70 years later of the fate of Lt. Tebo, my first American instructor at Grosse Ile, I was very upset, especially as I had been bombing Ishigaki Island around the same time as he was and had no idea that he was flying combat missions again in the Pacific War.'

APPENDICES

Appendix 1 Japanese Aircraft

Japanese aircraft code names that were given by the Americans and taken up to describe the aircraft. The fighters were given boy's names and the bombers given girl's names, and often referred to by the pilots when in combat or describing attacks on the ships by the Japanese aircraft. Here are some examples:

Army/Navy	Number	Type	Constructor	Crew	Year
Army					
Oscar	Ki-43	Fighter	Nakajima	1	1937
Tojo	Ki-44	Fighter	Nakajima	1	1941
Nick	Ki-45	Fighter	Kawasaki	2	1941
Tony	Ki-61	Fighter	Kawasaki	1	1943
Frank	Ki-84	Fighter	Nakajima	1	1943
Perry (last biplane)	Ki-10	Fighter	Kawasaki	1	1935
Navy					
Zeke	A6M	Fighter	Mitsubishi	1	1940
Jack	J2M	Fighter	Mitsubishi	1	1942
Rex	N1K	Fighter Seaplane	Kawanishi	1	1943
Army					
Sally	Ki-21	Bomber	Mitsubishi	5-7	1938
Lily	Ki-48	Bomber	Kawasaki	4-7	1940
Helen	Ki-49	Bomber	Nakajima	7	1941
Sonia	Ki-51	Bomber	Mitsubishi	2	1941
Navy					
Nell	G3M	Bomber	Mitsubishi	4-7	1935
Kate	B5N	Bomber	Nakajima	3	1937
Jill	B6N	Bomber	Nakajima	3	1937
Val	D3A	Bomber	Aichi	2	1940
Judy	D4Y	Bomber	Yokosuka	2	1942
Rufe	A6M2	Fighter Bomber	Nakajima	1	1942

Army					
Dinah	Ki-46	Reconnaissance	Mitsubishi	2	1939
Navy					
Mavis	H6K	Flying Boat	Kawanishi	8-10	1936
Jake	E13A	Floatplane	Aichi	3	1941
Myrt	C6N	Reconnaissance	Nakajima	1	1943

Japanese Training Aircraft

Designation	Model	Constructor	Type	Cockpit	Seats	Allied Codename
Ki-9	Army	Tachikawa	biplane	open	2	'Spruce'
Ki-17	Army	Tachikawa	biplane	open	2	'Cedar'
K5Y	Navy	Yokosuka	biplane	open	2	'Willow'
K3M	Navy	Mitsubishi	monoplane	enclosed	5 (Crew trainer)	'Pine'
Ki-55	Army	Tachikawa	monoplane	enclosed	2	'Ida'

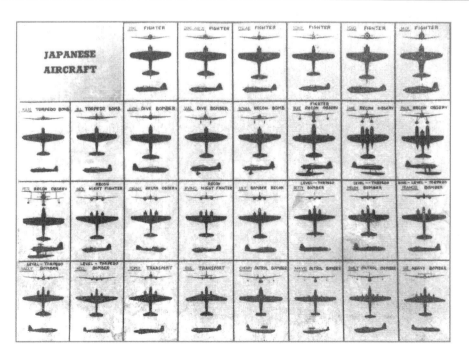

223

Appendix 2 American and British Aircraft

Fighters	Type	Constructor	Operation	Crew	RN Fleet Air Arm/Notes
Wildcat	F4F and FM	Grumman	1940	1	Known by RN FAA as the 'Martlet'
Hellcat	F6F	Grumman	1943	1	Known for a time as 'Gannet'
Corsair	F4U	Chance-Vought	1943	1	Known as Corsair I, II, III and IV
Firefly	Mk 1	Fairey	1943	2	Carrier aircraft in Pacific Theatre
Seafire	Mk III	Supermarine	1942	1	Carrier aircraft in Pacific Theatre
Lightning	P-38	Lockheed	1941	1	Shot down Adm. Yamamoto 'Betty'
Bombers					
Barracuda	Mk II	Fairey	1943	3	Was replaced by the Avenger
Avenger	TBF /TBM	Grumman	1942	3	Known as 'Tarpon' then 'Avenger'
Dauntless	SPD	Douglas	1941	2	9 supplied to FAA 1945-never used
Hell Diver	SB2C	Curtiss	1943	2	26 Supplied FAA-never used
Liberator	B-24	Consolidated	1941	12	Long-Range Bomber
Mitchell	B-25	North American	1941	3	Medium-Range/Ground Attack
Flying Fortress	B-17	Boeing	1941	10	Used by British Coastal Command

Super-fortress	B-29	Boeing	1943	10-14	'Enola Gay' -1st Atomic Bomb
Flying Boats					
PBY Catalina	PBY	Consolidated	1941	8	ASR /Reconnaissance
PBM Mariner	PBM	Martin	1940	7	ASR/Bomber /Transport
Walrus	Mk1 I/II	Supermarine	1939	4	ASR /Reconnaissance

Training Aircraft

Designation	Model	Constructor	Type	Cockpit	Seats	Other names
Tiger Moth		De Havilland	biplane	open	2	
NP1		Spartan	Biplane	Open	2	
N2S	Model 75	Boeing /Stearman	Biplane	Open	2	Kaydet /Yellow Peril
SNV	BT-13A	Vultee	Monoplane	Closed	2	Valiant
SNJ	AT6	North American	Monoplane	Closed	2	Texan/ Harvard
TBF	Avenger	Grumman	Monoplane	Closed	3	

Appendix 3

Memorial erected on Ishigaki to the Avenger crew executed by the Japanese

A memorial has been erected on the island of Ishigaki dedicated to Air Squadron VC97 Avenger crew: Lt. Vernon Tebo, Robert Tuggle Jnr and Warren H. Loyd. This was as a result of the dedicated work of Takeo Shinohara, a professor at the University of Ryukyus, and Air Force Technician Sgt. Tim Wilson, who was based at the Kadena Air Base.

Technical Sgt. Tim Wilson gathered a group of volunteers together to raise the funds to erect a memorial, while Professor Shinohara, along with the residents of Ishigaki, erected the memorial with the aim to ensure that the airmen were finally laid to rest.

The memorial dedication took place on August 15th 2001, and was attended by the families of men who died, the American Ambassador, the Mayor of Ishigaki, Professor Shinora, Technical Sgt. Tim Wilson and ex colleagues from VC-97 and the USS *Makassar Strait* CVE-91.

A memorial dedication was also held on June 16th 2011, at the National Museum of the Pacific War in Fredericksburg, Texas, to honour Lt. Vernon Tebo, Robert Tuggle and Warren H.Loyd.

Further details and photographs can be viewed on
www.shipleybay.com

Bibliography

Anthony J. The Royal Navy An Illustrated History. Brockhampton Press 1999.

Ashcroft, Dr. Bruce. We Wanted Wings: A History of the Aviation Cadet Program, Office of History and Research 2005

Brown, David. Carrier Operations in World War II Seaforth Publications 2009

Brown, David. Carrier Operations in World War II Volume II The Pacific Navies Dec 1941-Feb 1943 Ian Allen Ltd 1974

Brown, David. The Seafire The Spitfire that went to Sea Greenhill Books 1989

Brown, J.D. Carrier Operations in World War II Volume I The Royal Navy Ian Allan Ltd 1974

Crossley, Commander R. 'Mike', DSC, RN. They Gave Me a Seafire Airlife Publishing Ltd 1986

Eadon, Stuart. Kamikaze The Story of the British Pacific Fleet Crecy Books 1995

Eadon, Stuart. Sakishima Crecy Books 1995

Gunston, Bill. Allied Fighters of World War II. Salamander Books Ltd 1981

Hadley, Dunston. Barracuda Pilot Airlife Publishing ltd 2000

Hoyt, Edwin P. The Kamikazes Robert Hale Ltd 1983

Hoyt, Edwin P. Carrier Wars Robert Hale Ltd 1990

Jackson, Robert. Strike from the Sea Arthur Barker Ltd 1970

Keisel, Kenneth M and the Grosse Ile Historical Society. US Naval Air Station Grosse Ile. Arcadia Publishing 2011

Lamont-Brown, Raymond. Kamikaze Japan's Suicide Samurai Arms and Armour Press 1997

Lygo, Admiral Sir Raymond. Collision Course Lygo Shoots Back. The Book Guild Ltd 2002

Masatake Okumiya and Jiro Horikoshi with Martin Caiden. ZERO! The story of the Japanese Navy Air Force 1937-1945 Corgi Books 1958

Munson, Kenneth. Aircraft of World War II. Ian Allan Ltd 1972

Popham, Hugh. Sea Flight William Kimber and Co Ltd 1954

Rawlings, John D. R. Pictorial History of the Fleet Air Arm Ian Allan Ltd 1973

Roussel, Mike. Spitfire's Forgotten Designer: The career of Supermarine' Joe Smith. The History Press 2013

Samples, Fredio Wings over Sakishima Self Published 2010

Smith, Peter. Task Force 57 William Kimber and Co Ltd 1969

Stroud, John. Japanese Aircraft The Harborough Publishing Co Ltd 1945

Swanborough, Gordon and Bowers, Peter. United States Navy Aircraft since 1911 Putnam 1968

Turner, John Frayn. British Aircraft of World War II Sidgwick and Jackson 1975

Wragg, David. Fleet Air Arm Handbook 1939-1945 Sutton Publishing Ltd 2001

Other sources:

Before the Flying Tigers. Robert, E. van Patten. Air Force Magazine, 1999

Chapter 16 (232-51) Spitfire's Forgotten Designer: The career of Supermarine's Joe Smith. Mike Roussel

Innovation in Carrier Aviation, by Thomas C. Hone, Norman Friedman, and Mark D. Mandeles. Naval War College Press, Newport, Rhode Island 2011

IWM sound archives catalogue number 11294, 1990

IWM sound archives catalogue number 13858, 1994

IWM sound archives catalogue number 28723, 2006

IWM sound archives catalogue number 28938, 2006

Last Off, Last Back by Sub Lieutenant (A) Frank Stovin-Bradford. Aeroplane November and December 2002

Lt. Cdr. David Foster Obituary Daily Telegraph 18th July 2010

The London Gazette Supplement, Tuesday, 3rd April 1951.The Carrier-Borne

The London Gazette Supplement, Wednesday 2nd June, 1948.The Contribution of the British Pacific Fleet to the Assault of Okinawa, 1945

Websites, including:

www.royalnavyresearcharchive.org.uk

www.fleetairarm.com

www.iwm.org.uk

www.shipleybay.com

www.naval-history.net

www.1000aircraftphotos.com

www.maritimequest.com

www.joebaugher.com